ADEPTS,
MASTERS
and
MAHATMAS

Books by Harold W. Percival

THINKING AND DESTINY

MASONRY AND ITS SYMBOLS
In the Light of *Thinking and Destiny*

MAN AND WOMAN AND CHILD

DEMOCRACY IS SELF-GOVERNMENT

MONTHLY EDITORIALS FROM THE WORD 1904–1917 Part I

MONTHLY EDITORIALS FROM THE WORD 1904–1917 Part II

MOMENTS WITH FRIENDS FROM THE WORD 1906–1916

Editorial book series by topic from The Word *1904–1917:*

BROTHERHOOD / FRIENDSHIP

CHRIST / CHRISTMAS LIGHT

CYCLES / BIRTH-DEATH—DEATH-BIRTH

GLAMOUR / FOOD / THE VEIL OF ISIS

TWELVE PRINCIPLES OF THE ZODIAC

THE ZODIAC

I IN THE SENSES / PERSONALITY / SLEEP

CONSCIOUSNESS THROUGH KNOWLEDGE

PSYCHIC TENDENCIES AND DEVELOPMENT / DOUBT

KARMA

MIRRORS / SHADOWS

ADEPTS, MASTERS AND MAHATMAS

ATMOSPHERES / FLYING

HELL / HEAVEN

HOPE AND FEAR / WISHING / IMAGINATION

LIVING / LIVING FOREVER

INTOXICATIONS

GHOSTS

ADEPTS, MASTERS and MAHATMAS

Harold W. Percival

The Word Foundation, Inc.
PO Box 17510
Rochester, NY 14617
USA
thewordfoundation.org

TABLE OF CONTENTS

CONTENTS

LIST OF ILLUSTRATIONS

PREFACE

Harold W. Percival's monthly editorials were dictated by him and published in *The Word* magazine between October 1904 and September 1917. These editorials represent most of his early writings. For the following three decades, Percival devoted himself to what was to become his one-thousand-page masterpiece—*Thinking and Destiny*.

Adepts, Masters and Mahatmas is one in a series of eighteen compact books of Percival's editorials by topic. A complete list of these and all other books by Harold W. Percival is at the end of this book.

Whether you are new to H. W. Percival's early works or perhaps delighted to have them offered in two volumes or in eighteen smaller books by topic, we are pleased to make them available to you.

The Word Foundation

HAROLD W. PERCIVAL
1868 – 1953

OUR MESSAGE

[From *The Word,* Vol. 1 No. 1, October 1904]

This magazine is designed to bring to all who may read its pages, the message of the soul. The message is man is more than an animal in drapings of cloth—he is divine, though his divinity be masked by, and hidden in, the coils of flesh. Man is no accident of birth nor plaything of fate. He is a power, the creator and destroyer of fate. Through the power within, he will overcome indolence, outgrow ignorance, and enter the realm of wisdom. There he will feel a love for all that lives. He will be an everlasting power for good.

A bold message this. To some it will seem out of place in this busy world of change, confusion, vicissitudes, uncertainty. Yet we believe it is true, and by the power of truth it will live.

"It is nothing new," the modern philosopher may say, "ancient philosophies have told of this." Whatever the philosophies of the past may have said, modern philosophy has wearied the mind with learned speculations, which, continued on the material line, will lead to a barren waste. "Idle imagination," says the scientist of our day of materialism, failing to see the causes from which imagination springs. "Science gives me facts with which I can do something for those living in this world." Materialistic science may make of deserts fertile pastures, level mountains, and build great cities in the place of jungles. But science cannot remove the cause of restlessness and sorrow, sickness and disease, nor satisfy the yearnings of the soul. On the contrary, materialistic science would annihilate the soul, and resolve the universe into a cosmic dust heap. "Religion," says the theologian, thinking of his particular belief, "brings to the soul a message of peace and joy." Religions, so far, have shackled the mind; set man against man in the battle of life; flooded the earth with blood shed in religious sacrifices and spilled in wars. Given its own way, theology would make of its followers, idol-worshippers, put the Infinite in a form and endow it with human weakness.

Still, philosophy, science, and religion are the nurses, the teachers, the liberators of the soul. Philosophy is inherent in every human being; it is the love and yearning of the mind to open and embrace wisdom. By science the mind learns to relate things to each other, and to give them their proper places in the universe. Through religion, the mind becomes free from its sensuous bonds and is united with Infinite Being.

In the future, philosophy will be more than mental gymnastics, science will outgrow materialism, and religion will become unsectarian. In the future, man will act justly and will love his brother as himself, not because he longs for reward, or fears hell fire, or the laws of man: but because he will know that he is a part of his fellow, that he and his fellow are parts of a whole, and that whole is the One: that he cannot hurt another without hurting himself.

In the struggle for worldly existence, men trample on each other in their efforts to attain success. Having reached it at the cost of suffering and misery, they remain unsatisfied. Seeking an ideal, they chase a shadowy form. In their grasp, it vanishes.

Selfishness and ignorance make of life a vivid nightmare and of earth a seething hell. The wail of pain mingles with the laughter of the gay. Fits of joy are followed by spasms of distress. Man embraces and clings closer to the cause of his sorrows, even while held down by them. Disease, the emissary of death, strikes at his vitals. Then is heard the message of the soul. This message is of strength, of love, of peace. This is the message we would bring: the strength to free the mind from ignorance, prejudice, and deceit; the courage to seek the truth in every form; the love to bear each other's burdens; the peace that comes to a freed mind, an opened heart, and the consciousness of an undying life.

Let all who receive *The Word* pass on this message. Each one who has something to give which will benefit others is invited to contribute to its pages.

———————————

ADEPTS, MASTERS AND MAHATMAS

[From *The Word,* Vol. 9 No. 4, July 1909]

THESE words have been in general use for many years. The first two come from the Latin, the last from the Sanscrit. Adept is a word which has been in popular use for many centuries and has been applied in many ways. It was, however, used in a particular way by the mediaeval alchemists, who in using the term, meant one who had attained to the knowledge of the alchemical art, and who was proficient in the practice of alchemy. In common use, the term was applied to anyone who was proficient in his art or profession. The word master has been in common use from early times. It is derived from the Latin magister, a ruler, and has been used as a title to indicate one who had authority over others by reason of employment or power, as the head of a family, or as a teacher. It was given a special place in the terminology of the alchemists and rosicrucians of mediaeval times as meaning one who had become master of his subject, and who was capable of directing and instructing others. The term mahatma is a Sanscrit word, the common meaning being great soul, from maha, great, and atma, soul, dating back many thousands of years. It has not, however, been incorporated into the English language until recent times, but may now be found in lexicons.

The term mahatma is now applied in its native country as well to anyone who is considered great in soul as to Indian fakirs and yogis. In the occident, the word is usually applied to those who are considered to have attained the highest degree of adeptship. So these terms have been in common use for hundreds and for thousands of years. A special meaning has been given to them within the last thirty-five years.

Since the founding of the Theosophical Society in 1875 in New York by Madam Blavatsky, these terms, through the use by her, have assumed somewhat different and more pointed meaning than before. Madam Blavatsky said that she had been instructed by adepts, masters or mahatmas to form a society for the purpose of making known to the world certain teachings concerning God, Nature and Man, which teachings the world had forgotten or was not aware of. Madam Blavatsky stated that the adepts, masters and mahatmas of whom she spoke were men possessed of the highest wisdom, who had a knowledge of the laws of life and death, and of the phenomena of nature, and who were able to control the forces of nature and produce phenomena according to natural law as they desired. She said that these adepts, masters and mahatmas from whom she received her knowledge were located in the East, but that they existed in all parts of the world, though unknown to mankind in general. Further it was said by Madam Blavatsky that all adepts, masters and mahatmas were or had been men, who through long ages and by continuous effort had succeeded in mastering, dominating and controlling their lower nature and who were able and did act according to the knowledge and wisdom to which they had attained. In the Theosophical Glossary, written by Madam Blavatsky, we find the following:

"Adept. (Lat.) Adeptus, 'He who has attained.' In Occultism one who has reached the stage of Initiation, and become a Master in the science of Esoteric philosophy."

"Mahâtma. Lit., 'great soul.' An adept of the highest order. Exalted beings who, having attained to the mastery over their lower principles are thus living unimpeded by the 'man of flesh,' and are in possession of knowledge and power commensurate with the stage they have reached in their spiritual evolution."

In the volumes of "The Theosophist" and of "Lucifer" prior to 1892, Madam Blavatsky has written a great deal concerning adepts, masters and mahatmas. Since then a considerable literature has been developed through the Theosophical Society and in which many uses have been made of these terms. But Blavatsky is the authority and witness before the world as to the existence of the beings of whom she spoke as adepts, masters and mahatmas. These terms have been used by theosophists and others in a different sense than the meaning given them by Blavatsky. Of this we will speak later. All those, however, who came in contact with and accepted the doctrines given by her and who then spoke and later wrote concerning adepts, masters and mahatmas confessedly obtained their knowledge of them from her. Madam Blavatsky by her teachings and writings has given evidence of some source of knowledge from which came the teachings known as theosophical.

While Madam Blavatsky and those who understood her teaching have written about adepts, masters and mahatmas, there has been not much definite nor direct information given as to the particular meaning of each as distinguished from the other of these terms, nor about the position and stages which these beings fill in evolution. Owing to the use made of the terms by Madam Blavatsky and the Theosophical Society, these terms have then been adopted by others who, with many theosophists, use the terms as synonymous and in a confused and indiscriminate manner. So there is an ever-increasing need of information as to whom and what the terms mean, for what, where, when, and how, the beings whom they represent exist.

If there are such beings as adepts, masters and mahatmas, then they must occupy a definite place and stage in evolution, and this place and stage must be found in every system or plan which deals truly with God, Nature and Man. There is a system which is furnished by nature, the plan of which is in man. This system or plan is known as the zodiac. The zodiac of which we speak, however, are not the constellations in the heavens known by this term, though these twelve constellations symbolize our zodiac. Neither do we speak of the zodiac in the sense in which it is used by modern astrologers. The system of the zodiac of which we speak has been outlined in many editorials which have appeared in *The Word* [*pp. 4–169 in* The Zodiac *in this book series*].

It will be found by consulting these articles that the zodiac is symbolized by a circle, which in turn stands for a sphere. The circle is divided by a horizontal line; the upper half is said to represent the unmanifested and the lower half the manifested universe. The seven signs from cancer (♋) to capricorn (♑) below the horizontal line relate to the manifested universe. The signs above the middle horizontal line are symbols of the unmanifested universe.

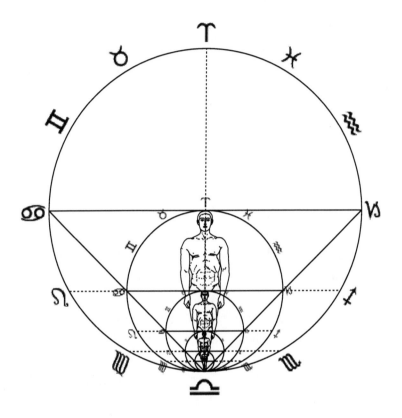

FIGURE 30

    The manifested universe of seven signs is divided into four worlds or spheres which, beginning with the lowest, are the physical, the astral or psychic, the mental and the spiritual spheres or worlds. These worlds are considered from an involutionary and evolutionary standpoint. The first world or sphere called into existence is the spiritual, which is on the line or plane, cancer—capricorn (♋ – ♑) and in its involutionary aspect is the breath world, cancer (♋). The next is the life world, leo (♌); the next is the form world, virgo (♍); and the lowest is the physical sex world, libra (♎). This is the plan of involution. The complement to and completion of these worlds is seen in their evolutionary aspects. The signs which correspond to and complete those mentioned are scorpio (♏), sagittary (♐), and capricorn (♑). Scorpio (♏), desire, is the attainment reached in the form world, (♍–♏); thought (♐), is the control of the life world (♌–♐); and individuality, capricorn (♑), is the completion and perfection of the breath, the spiritual world (♋–♑). The spiritual, mental and astral worlds are equilibrated and balanced in and through the physical world, libra (♎).

Each world has its own beings who are conscious of their being in the particular world to which they belong and in which they live. In involution, the beings of the breath world, those of the life world, those in the form world, and those in the physical world were each conscious of its particular world, but each class or kind in its world was not or is not conscious of those in either of the other worlds. As for instance, the strictly physical man is not conscious of the astral forms which are within him and which surround him, nor of the sphere of life in which he lives and which pulses through him, nor of the spiritual breaths which endow him with his distinctive being and in and by which perfectibility is possible for him. All of these worlds and principles are within and around physical man, as they are within and around the physical world. The purpose of evolution is that all these worlds and their intelligent principles should be equilibrated by and act intelligently through the physical body of man, so that man within his physical body should be conscious of all the manifested worlds and be able to act intelligently in any or all of the worlds while still in his physical body. To do this steadily and continuously, man must make for himself a body for each of the worlds; each body must be of the material of the world in which he is to act intelligently. In the present stage of evolution, man has within him the principles which have been named; that is to say, he is a spiritual breath through a pulsing life in a definite form within his physical body acting in the physical world. But he is conscious of his physical body only, and of the physical world only because he has built no permanent body or form for himself. He is conscious of the physical world and his physical body now because he is functioning in the physical body here and now. He is conscious of his physical body so long as it lasts and no longer; and inasmuch as the physical world and the physical body are only a world and a body of equilibrium and balance, he is therefore unable to build a physical body to last through the change of time. He continues to build physical bodies one after the other through numerous lives in which he lives for a short span, and at the death of each he withdraws into the state of sleep or rest in the form world or in the world of thought without having equilibrated his principles and found himself. He comes again into the physical and will so continue to come life after life until he shall establish for himself a body or bodies other than physical, in which he may live consciously in or out of the physical.

Mankind now lives in physical bodies and is conscious of the physical world only. In future mankind will still live in physical bodies, but men will grow out of the physical world and be conscious of each of the other worlds as they build a body or garment or vesture with or through which they may act in those worlds.

The terms adept, master and mahatma represent the stages or degrees of each of the other three worlds. These stages are marked according to the degree by the signs or symbols of the universal plan of the zodiac.

An adept is one who has learned to make use of the inner senses analogous to that of the physical senses and who can act in and through the inner senses in the world of forms and desires. The difference is that whereas man acts through his senses in the physical world and perceives through his senses things which are tangible to the physical senses, the adept uses senses of sight, hearing, smelling, tasting and touching in the world of forms and desires, and that whereas the forms and desires could not be seen nor sensed by the physical body, he is now able by the cultivation and development of the inner senses, to perceive and deal with the desires acting through form which desires impelled the physical to action. The adept as such acts in a body of form similar to the physical, but the form is known to be what it is according to the nature and degree of its desire and is known to all who can act intelligently on the astral planes. That is to say, as any intelligent man may tell the race and rank and degree of culture of any other physical man, so any adept may know the nature and degree of any other adept which he may meet in the form–desire world. But whereas one living in the physical world may deceive another man in the physical world, as to his race and position, no one in the form–desire world can deceive an adept as to his nature and degree. In physical life the physical body is held intact in form by the form which gives the matter shape, and this physical matter in form is impelled to action by desire. In physical man the form is distinct and defined, but the desire is not. The adept is one who has built a body of desire, which body of desire may either act through his astral form or by itself as a body of desire, to which he has given form. The ordinary man of the physical world has plenty of desire, but this desire is a blind force. The adept has moulded the blind force of desire into form, which is no longer blind, but has senses corresponding to those of the form body, which act through the physical body. An adept, therefore, is one who has attained to the use and function of his desires in a form body apart from or independent of the physical body. The sphere or world in which the adept as such functions is the astral or psychic world of form, on the plane of virgo–scorpio (♍–♏), form–desire, but he acts from the point of scorpio (♏) desire. An adept has attained to the full action of desire. The adept as such is a body of desire acting in a form apart from the physical. The characteristics of an adept are that he deals with phenomena, such as the producing of forms, the changing of forms, the summoning of forms, the compelling to action of forms, all of which is controlled by the power of desire, as he acts from desire on forms and things of the sense world.

A master is one who has related and balanced the sex nature of the physical body, who has overcome his desires and the matter of the form world, and who controls and directs the matter of the life world on the plane of leo–sagittary (♌–♐) from his position and by the power of thought, sagittary (♐). An adept is one who, by the power of desire, has attained to free action in the form–desire world, separate and apart from the physical body. A master is one who has mastered the physical appetites, the force of desire, who has control of the currents of life, and who has done this by the power of thought from his position in the mental world of thought. He is a master of life and has evolved a body of thought and may live in this thought body clear and free from his desire body and physical body, though he may live in or act through either or both. The physical man deals with objects, the adept deals with desires, a master deals with thought. Each acts from his own world. The physical man has senses which attract him to the objects of the world, the adept has transferred his plane of action but still has the senses corresponding to those of the physical; but a master has overcome and risen above both to the ideals of life from which the senses and desires and their objects in the physical are mere reflections. As objects are in the physical and desires are in the form world, so thoughts are in the life world. Ideals are in the mental thought world what desires are in the form world and objects in the physical world. As an adept sees desires and forms invisible to the physical man, so a master sees and deals with thoughts and ideals which are not perceived by the adept, but which may be apprehended by the adept similarly to the manner in which the physical man senses desire and form which is not physical. As desire is not distinctive in form in the physical man, but is so in the adept, so in the adept thought is not distinct, but thought is a distinctive body of a master. As an adept has full command and action of desire apart from the physical which the physical man has not, so a master has the full and free action and power of thought in a body of thought which the adept has not. The characteristic features of a master are that he deals with life and the ideals of life. He directs and controls the currents of life according to ideals. He so acts with life as a master of life, in a thought body and by the power of thought.

A mahatma is one who has overcome, grown out of, lived through and risen above the sex world of physical man, the form–desire world of the adept, the life–thought world of the master and is acting freely in the spiritual breath world as a fully conscious and immortal individual, having the right to be entirely freed and apart from or be connected with or act through the thought body, the desire body and the physical body. A mahatma is the perfection and completion of evolution. Breath was the beginning of the involution of the manifested worlds for the education and perfection of mind. Individuality is the end of the evolution and perfection of mind. A mahatma is such full and complete development of individuality or mind, which marks the end and accomplishment of evolution.

A mahatma is an individualized mind free from the necessity of further contact with any of the worlds lower than the spiritual breath world. A mahatma deals with breath according to the law by which all things are breathed into manifestation from the unmanifested universe, and by which all things manifested are breathed again into the unmanifested. A mahatma deals with ideas, the eternal verities, the realities of ideals, and according to which the sensuous worlds appear and disappear. As objects and sex in the physical world, and the senses in the desire world, and ideals in the thought world, cause action by the beings in those worlds, so are ideas the eternal laws according to which and by which mahatmas act in the spiritual breath world.

An adept is not free from reincarnation because he has not overcome desire and is not freed from virgo and scorpio. A master has overcome desire, but may not be freed from the necessity to reincarnate because whereas he has mastered his body and desires he may not have worked out all of the karma connected with his past thoughts and actions, and where it is not possible for him to work out in his present physical body all of the karma which he has engendered in the past, it will be incumbent on him to reincarnate in as many bodies and conditions as will be necessary that he may fully and completely work out his karma according to the law. A mahatma differs from the adept and the master in that the adept must still reincarnate because he is still making karma, and a master must reincarnate because, although he is no longer making karma he is working out that which he has already made, but the mahatma, having ceased to make karma and having worked out all karma, is entirely freed from any necessity to reincarnate. The meaning of the word mahatma makes this clear. Ma indicates manas, the mind. Ma is the individual ego or mind, while mahat is the universal principle of mind. Ma, the individual mind, acts within mahat, the universal principle. This universal principle includes all the manifested universe and its worlds. Ma is the principle of mind which is individual as distinct from, though it is within the universal mahat; but ma must become a complete individuality, which it is not in the beginning. In the beginning the ma, a mind, acts from the spiritual world of breath at the sign cancer (♋), breath, and there remains until by involution and the development of other principles the lowest point of the involution is reached at libra (♎), the physical world of sex, from which point the other principles necessary to the development and perfection of mind are to be evolved. The ma or mind acts within the mahat or universal mind through all its phases of involution and by evolution until it emerges and rises plane by plane, world by world, to the plane on the rising arc corresponding to the plane from which it started on the descending arc. It began its descent at cancer (♋); the lowest point reached was libra (♎); from there it began its ascent and rises to capricorn (♑), which is the end of its journey and is the same plane from which it descended. It was ma, the mind, in the beginning of involution at cancer (♋); it is ma, the mind, at the end of evolution at capricorn (♑). But the ma has passed through mahat, and is a mahat-ma. That is to say, the mind has passed through all phases and degrees of the universal mind, mahat, and having united with it and at the same time completed its full individuality is, therefore, a mahatma.

(To be continued)

ADEPTS, MASTERS AND MAHATMAS

(Continued)

[From *The Word,* Vol. 9 No. 5, August 1909]

THERE are many objections as to the existence of adepts, masters and mahatmas naturally arising in the minds of those who hear of the subject for the first time, or who having heard of it consider it irrational and preposterous, or as a scheme to delude the people and to obtain their money, or to gain notoriety and a following. According to their different natures, the objectors mildly pronounce against such belief or vehemently declare it to be a worship of false gods or attempt to wither with their sarcasm and ridicule those who announce their belief in the teaching, while others find opportunity to display their fine wit, and they joke and laugh about the doctrine. Others, on hearing it for the first time or after consideration of the subject, believe it naturally and declare the doctrine to be reasonable and necessary in the scheme of universal evolution.

Among the objections raised is one that if adepts, masters or mahatmas exist, then why do they not themselves come among mankind instead of sending an emissary to declare their existence. The reply is that the mahatma as such is a being not of the physical, but of the spiritual world, and it is not fit that he should himself come to give his message when another in the world can carry that message. In the same manner in which the governor or ruler of a city or country does not himself communicate laws to the artisans or merchants or citizens, but communicates such laws by an intermediary, so a mahatma as an agent of the universal law does not himself go to the people of the world to communicate universal laws and principles of right action, but sends an emissary to advise or remind the people of the laws under which they live. Citizens might declare that the governor of a state should communicate with them directly, but the governor would pay little attention to such statements, knowing that those who made them did not understand the office which he filled and the purpose which he served. A mahatma will pay as little attention to those who think it his duty to bring his message and show himself to prove his existence, as the governor would in the case of ignorant citizens. But the mahatma would nevertheless continue to act as he knew best, notwithstanding such objections. It might be said the illustration does not hold because the governor could prove his existence and his position by appearing before the people and by the records and by those who witnessed his inauguration, whereas the people have never seen a mahatma and have no proof of his existence. This is true in part only. The message of a governor and the message of a mahatma is the essence or substance of the message as it affects or is related to those to whom it is given. The personality of the governor or individuality of the mahatma is of secondary importance as compared with the message. The governor can be seen, because he is a physical being, and the body of a mahatma cannot be seen because a mahatma is not physical, but is a spiritual being, though he may have a physical body. The governor may prove to the people that he is the governor, because the physical records show that he is and other physical men will bear witness to the fact. This cannot be the case with a mahatma, not because there are not records and witnesses of the fact, but because the records of the becoming of a mahatma are not physical, and physical men, while they are only physical, cannot examine such records.

Another objection raised against the existence of mahatmas is that if they do exist and have the knowledge and power claimed for them, then why do they not solve the social, political and religious problems of the day about which the whole world is disturbed and confused. We answer, for the same reason that a teacher does not at once solve the problem over which a child is puzzled, but assists the child to solve its problem by pointing out the rules of the problem and the principles by which it may be worked out. If the teacher were to solve the problem for the child, the child would not learn its lesson and would have gained nothing by the operation. No wise teacher will solve a problem for a scholar before that scholar has worked over the problem and shows by the steadiness and earnestness of his work that he desires to learn. A mahatma will not solve the modern problems because these are the very lessons by which humanity is learning and the learning of which will make responsible men. In the same manner in which the teacher gives advice to the pupil who is puzzled over a difficult and critical stage in a problem, so the adepts, masters and mahatmas do give advice to humanity through the means they see fit, whenever a race or people show their earnest desire to master the problem with which they are concerned. The pupil often refuses the teacher's advice and will not work according to a rule or principle suggested by the teacher. So also may a race or people refuse to work out their problem according to certain rules or principles of life suggested by an adept, master or mahatma, through such intermediary as he might select to give his advice. A master would not insist then, but would wait until the people he had advised should be willing to learn. It is asked that a mahatma should decide the question and enforce by his knowledge and power that which he knows to be right and best. So he might, according to his power; but he knows better. A mahatma will not break the law. If a mahatma inaugurated a certain form of government or state of society which he knew to be best, but which the people did not understand, he would have to compel the people to act and to perform functions which they would not understand because they had not learned. By so doing he would act against the law, whereas he desires to teach them to live in conformity with law and not against it.

Humanity is at an important point in its development. Mankind is much disturbed over its problems, as a child over its lessons. At this important juncture in the history of the race the mahatmas have offered to mankind such rules and principles of life as will solve their vexed problems. It remains to be seen whether mankind will, like a ready scholar, act on the principles and advice offered, or whether they will refuse the advice and continue to fumble on over their problems in a confused and distracted manner.

Another objection is that if the beings called mahatmas, whether they be facts or fancies, are exalted to the plane claimed for them, this gives them the place of God and does away with the worship of the true God.

This objection can be raised only by one who believes that his god is the true God. The mahatmas of whom we speak do not desire the worship of mankind. The mahatmas of whom we speak are better than any of the gods who demand worship of their followers. The real God of the universe cannot be ousted from its place, nor would a mahatma wish to put out of place the one God, were that possible. The mahatmas of whom we speak will not appear to men, because such appearance would excite human beings and cause them to worship them without knowing really what they worshipped. The mahatmas of whom we speak do not enter into competition for the worship or adoration of human beings, as do, according their respective theologies, the different gods of the different religions, each of which claims as the one true and only god, the particular god whom they worship. One who would worship a mahatma or a god proclaims positively by his action that he has no comprehension of the one God through all.

Adepts, masters and mahatmas are necessary links in the plan of evolution. Each has his place in the different planes of being. Each is an intelligence working consciously in the astral, the mental and spiritual worlds. The adept is the conscious link between the physical and the mental. He lives consciously in the astral world. A master is the conscious link between the astral and the spiritual worlds. He lives consciously in the mental or thought world. A mahatma is the conscious link between the mental world and the unmanifested. He lives consciously and intelligently in the spiritual world. Were it not for the intelligences here named adepts, masters and mahatmas, each acting consciously on the unintelligent matter, forces, beings, in his own world, it would be impossible for that which is unmanifested to become manifest to the senses in the physical world and for that which is now manifest to pass again into the unmanifested.

Adepts, masters and mahatmas, each acting from his own world, are intelligent agents of the universal law. The adept acts with forms and desires, and their transformation. A master acts with life and thoughts and their ideals. A mahatma deals with ideas, the realities of ideals.

Adepts, masters and mahatmas are the logical sequence and results of repeated reincarnations. One who believes that the mind reincarnates in physical human forms cannot reasonably suppose that it will continue to do so without acquiring a greater knowledge of life and of the laws of life. He cannot fail to see that at some time in its reincarnations, the mind will come into possession of greater knowledge as the result of its efforts to acquire knowledge. Such knowledge will be used as the means to a growth out of or beyond the limitations of the body. The result is adeptship. As the adept continues to advance in knowledge, to control his desires and to transform lower into higher forms, he comes into possession of a greater knowledge of life and the wonders of thought. He enters consciously into the world of thought and becomes a master of life and of thought. As he progresses he rises into the spiritual world and becomes a mahatma, and is an immortal, intelligent and individualized mind. Adepts, masters and mahatmas are necessary not only to assist the individual members of humanity, but to act with the elemental forces in all nature. They are the links, mediators, transmitters, interpreters, of divinity and nature to man.

History lacks evidence of the existence of adepts, masters and mahatmas in so far as it records the lives and characters of the makers of history. Although adepts, masters or mahatmas may have taken part in historical events and may even have been historical characters, they were disinclined to have themselves known or to appear as different from others. They have seldom allowed themselves to be spoken of by these or similar terms. In fact those who have allowed themselves to be called by the name, adept, master, or mahatma, were least deserving of the term and of what the title implied, excepting the cases of the founders of great religions and the individualities around whom great religions have been built.

Although history does not contain many records of such beings it does mention the lives of some men whose lives and teachings give evidence that they were beyond the ordinary human being: that they were possessed of a knowledge far exceeding human knowledge, that they were divine, that they were conscious of their divinity and that divinity shone through them and was exemplified in their lives.

The name of one of each class will suffice to illustrate. Apollonius of Tyana was an adept. He possessed a knowledge of elemental forces and could control some of them. The history of his time records that he could appear in two places simultaneously; that he did many times appear in places where others did not see him enter and that he disappeared at times when those present did not see him depart.

Pythagoras of Samos was a master. He was acquainted with and did control, as a master, most of the forces and powers with which an adept deals; as a master he dealt with the lives and thoughts and ideals of humanity. He founded a school in which he taught his pupils concerning the laws and forms of thought, demonstrated to them the means by which their thoughts might be controlled, their ideals elevated and their aspirations attained. He knew the law concerning the conduct of human life and the harmonies of thought, and assisted his pupils in becoming masters also of their thoughts and lives. So thoroughly did he impress his great knowledge on the thought of the world that by what he taught and left through the works of his pupils, the world has been benefited, and will be benefited, in proportion as it is able to understand the profound problems which he undertook to teach. His system of politics and his philosophy of numbers, of the movements of bodies in space and of universal motions, are comprehended in proportion to the greatness of those minds who struggle with the problems which he had mastered and taught.

Gautama of Kapilavastu was a mahatma. He possessed not only knowledge and control of the elemental forces and had ceased to make karma by which he would be bound to reincarnate, but he worked out in that life through his physical body the effects remaining over from previous lives. He could consciously, intelligently and at will, pass into or know any thing concerning any or all of the manifested worlds. He lived and acted in the physical, he moved in and controlled the powers of the astral, he sympathized with and guided the thoughts and ideals of the mental, he knew and realized the ideas of the spiritual, and was able to act consciously in all these worlds. As an individual mind, he had lived through all phases of the universal mind and having attained to a perfect knowledge of all phases of the universal mind, passed into or beyond it and was therefore a mahat-ma.

The three, Apollonius, the adept; Pythagoras, the master, and Gautama, the mahat-ma, are known in history by their physical appearance and by their action in and on the world and with man. They may be known by other means and by other faculties than those of the physical senses. But until we have the means and develop such faculties, we cannot know them except by judging their actions. Physical man is such by virtue of physical matter; the adept is an adept by virtue of a body with which he may work in the invisible astral world as the physical body works with things physical; a master is such by means of his having a definite and positive body of the nature and quality of the thought with which he works; the mahatma is such by virtue of his having a definite and immortal individuality of mind with which he knows and by which he executes the law according to universal justice and being.

History cannot record the existence and life of these men because history leaves a record of such events only as occur in the physical world. Evidences of the existence of such intelligences are given by the events which were brought about by the presence of such intelligences acting through the thoughts and desires of a people and leaving their mark in the lives of men. Such evidences we find in the great teachings left us by the sages of the past, by the philosophies built up and religions founded by these great men themselves or from and around the doctrines which they have left to mankind. An adept, master or mahatma gives to a people a philosophy or a religion which that people is most ready to receive. When they have outgrown the teachings or ethics given them or when the development of the minds of the people requires a different presentation of even the same doctrines, an adept, master or mahatma furnishes a teaching which is best suited to the natural development of the people's mind or such religion as the desires of a people long for.

Among the first questions which arise in the mind of one who hears of or is interested in the subject of adepts, masters and mahatmas is this: if such beings exist, where do they live, physically? Legend and myth say that wise men forsake the haunts of men and have their habitations in mountains, forests, deserts and places far removed. Madam Blavatsky said that many of them lived in the

Himalaya mountains, in the Gobi desert and in certain other unfrequented parts of the earth. On hearing them thus located, the man of the world even though he may have been inclined to consider the subject favorably will become doubtful, sceptical and will laughingly say: why not put them in the sky, at the bottom of the deep sea or in the interior of the earth, where they would be still more inaccessible. The keener his mind, and the more familiar a man is with the ways of the world, the more suspicious will he become of the sanity or honesty of the person or set of people who speak of adepts, masters or mahatmas and tell of their wonderful powers.

There are frauds among those who talk about adepts, masters and mahatmas as there are among priests and preachers. These the man of the world and the materialist see. Yet the materialist does not understand the power which moves in the heart of the religious man and causes him to hold to his religion in preference to the crumbs of science. Nor can the worldly wise understand why people should believe in adepts, masters and mahatmas placed so far away instead of living in places easy of access. There is something in the heart of the religious man which draws him to religion as a magnet draws the iron, and there is that in the heart of the one who honestly believes in adepts, masters and mahatmas which urges him on, even though he may not be aware of it, to the path of sympathy and knowledge to which adepts, masters and mahatmas as ideals lead the way.

Not all adepts, masters and mahatmas have their habitations in inaccessible places, but when they have there is a reason for it. Adepts may move and live among men and even in the noise and bustle of a city because the duties of an adept often bring him into the maelstrom of human life. A master would not live in the noise and bustle of a large city though he may be near one, because his work is not in the whirlpool of desires and forms, but with the purer life and with the ideals and thoughts of men. A mahatma need not and could not live in the market place or the highways of the world because his work is with realities and is removed from the quarrels and confusion of desires and changing ideals and is concerned with the permanent and the true.

When one stops to think of the nature, development and the place in evolution which the adepts, masters and mahatmas must fill, if such beings do exist, the objections to the inaccessibility of their habitation, appear to be unworthy of a thoughtful mind.

No one thinks it strange that the faculty of a college requires quiet in the class room, because we know that quiet is necessary to profitable study, and no one except the teacher and the students are concerned in the studies of the class while it is in session. No person of intelligence wonders that the astronomer builds his observatory on the top of a mountain in a clear atmosphere instead of in the busy streets in the sink of a city, in an air filled with smoke and gloom, because he knows that the astronomer's business is concerned with the stars and that he cannot observe these and follow their motions if their light is shut off from his vision by smoke and his mind is disturbed by the din and turmoil of the street.

If we allow that quiet and solitude are necessary to the astronomer, and that those not concerned with the work should not be present during important observations, it would be absurd to suppose that those having no right would be admitted to the fastnesses of a mahatma, or be allowed to look on while he communed with intelligences in the spiritual world and guided the destinies of nations as determined by their own actions and according to the inexorable laws of right and justice.

One might object to the analogies used and say that we do know that teachers of colleges exist because thousands of men and women have been taught by them and large edifices bear witness of their office; that we do know that astronomers live and work because they give the results of their observations to the world, and we may read of their work in the books which they have written; whereas, we have nothing to prove the existence of adepts, masters and mahatmas, because we have nothing to show that they act in capacities similar to the teacher or the astronomer.

What makes the physician a physician, the teacher a teacher, the astronomer an astronomer? and what makes the adept an adept, the master a master, the mahatma a mahatma? The physician or surgeon is such because of his familiarity with the body, his acquaintance with medicine, and his skill in the treatment and cure of disease; the teacher is such because he has learned the rules of speech, is acquainted with the sciences, and is able to and does impart information thereof to other minds who are able to embrace it. A man is an astronomer because of his knowledge of the laws governing the movements of the heavenly bodies, his skill and accuracy in observations following their movements and in his ability to record such observations and predict celestial phenomena according to law. Usually we think of the professions as intelligent physical bodies. This is an erroneous notion. We cannot put our hands on the skill of the physician, the learning of the teacher, nor the knowledge of the astronomer. Nor can we hold the astral body of the adept, the power of thought of a master, nor the immortal being of a mahatma.

It is true that we can put our hands on the bodies of physicians, teachers and astronomers. It is just as true that we could do the same with adepts, masters and some mahatmas. But we can no more touch the real physician, teacher or astronomer, than we can the real adept, master or mahatma.

Adepts, masters and mahatmas may and do have physical bodies as have physicians, teachers and astronomers. But not everybody would be able to point out the physicians, teachers and astronomers in a crowd, any more than he would be able to distinguish adepts, masters and mahatmas from other men. Physicians, teachers or astronomers do look somewhat different than farmers and sailors and one who is familiar with the professions would be able to distinguish a type of a physician from those who are unlike him, and to tell the characteristic schoolman. But in order to do so he must be familiar with these professions or have seen these men at their work. Their work and thought lends character and habit to their appearance and movement of body. The same may be said of adepts, masters and mahatmas. Unless we are familiar with the work and thought and knowledge of adepts, masters and mahatmas we can not distinguish them as such from other men.

There are as many evidences of the existence of adepts, masters and mahatmas, as there are of physicians, teachers and astronomers, but in order to see the evidences we must be able to recognize them as evidences when we do see them.

The universe is a great machine. It is composed of certain parts, each of which performs a function in the general economy of action. In order that this huge machine be kept running and in repair it must have competent machinists and engineers, able and skillful chemists, intelligent scribes and exact mathematicians.

One who has passed through a large printing establishment and has seen a typesetting machine and large cylinder press in operation would reject the suggestion that the typesetting machine or printing press could have been evolved and be kept running without any guiding intelligences. The typesetting machine and printing press are wonderful machines; but the universe or a human body is infinitely more wonderful than either of these intricate and delicately adjusted inventions of the human mind. If we should scout the notion that a typesetting machine or a printing press could have happened to be as they are without human intervention, and that the typesetter would set type and the printing press print it into a book intelligently written without human aid, why should we not also scout the suggestion that the universe was simply evolved from chaos into its present form without guiding intelligences and builders, or that the bodies moving through space in a harmonious and rhythmic order and according to definite and unvarying law should continue to be so moved without intelligences to guide or direct the unintelligent matter.

This world does more wonderful things requiring intelligence than the setting of type or the printing of a book without human hands or human mind. The world develops the different kinds of minerals and metals within her body by definite laws, though unknown to man. She pushes up the blade of grass and the lily; these take on colors and give forth odors and wither and die and are reproduced again, all according to fixed definite laws of season and place, though unknown to man. She causes mating, the gestation of life, and the birth of animal and human bodies, all according to definite laws but little known to man. The world is kept revolving in and through space by its own motion and other motions which man knows little about; and the forces or laws of heat, light, gravitation, electricity, become wonderful and more mysterious as they are studied, though as laws in themselves they remain unknown to man. If intelligence and human agencies are necessary in the construction and operation of a typesetting machine and printing press, how much more necessary must be the existence of adepts, masters and mahatmas, as beings of intelligence who fill offices and positions in the economy of nature and act with and according to the laws by which the universe is maintained and operated. Adepts, masters and mahatmas must of necessity exist in the present as they have in the past in order that the organism of nature might be kept in repair and continue in operation, that the power which impels the machine might be supplied and directed, that the unformed elements might be fabricated and given form, that gross material may be turned out into finished products, that animal creation might be guided into higher forms, that the ungoverned desires and thoughts of men might be turned into higher aspirations and that the human who lives and dies and comes again might become one of the intelligent and immortal host who aid in the carrying out of law, which operates in every department of nature and of human life.

(To be continued)

ADEPTS, MASTERS AND MAHATMAS

(Continued)

[From *The Word,* Vol. 9 No. 6, September 1909]

MAHATMAS do live apart from ordinary men, not because they dislike or have grown apart from them, but because it is necessary that their habitations are far from the atmosphere of the market place. The dwelling place of a master is also removed from the rush of life and desires in a large city, because his work is not in a maelstrom of desires of physical existence, but with orderly systems of thought. The adept, too, seeks a habitation away from the cauldron of physical life, because his studies must be conducted quietly, but when necessary he enters into and may live an entire life busily engaged with affairs of the world. The adept is particularly concerned with forms and desires and the customs of men and with the changes of these; therefore he must at times be in the world.

Adepts, masters and mahatmas do not choose their physical abodes because of likes or prejudices, but because it is often necessary for them to live and act from certain points on the earth's surface which are best suited for their work. Before selecting a physical habitation and center from which their work is to be done, they must consider many factors, among them, magnetic centers of the earth, freedom from or prevailing of elemental conditions, the clearness, density or lightness of the atmosphere, the position of the earth in relation to sun and moon, the influence of the moonlight and sunlight.

There are seasons and cycles in which the races of man and his civilizations come and go in each age of the earth. These races and civilizations appear and proceed around the earth's surface within a zone. The path of the centers of civilization is like that of a serpent.

There are geographical centers on the earth's surface which have served as the stages on which the drama-comedy-tragedy of life has been enacted again and again. Within the serpentine path of civilization is the zone of human progression, while those not belonging to the age may live on the borders of or away from the zone. Adepts, masters and mahatmas select their habitations, with respect to the progress of man, along this path of civilization. They live at such points on the earth's surface as will enable them to deal best with those with whom they are concerned. Their dwellings away from men are naturally in caves and forests and on mountains and in deserts.

Caves are chosen, among other reasons, because in their recesses bodies undergoing certain initiations are protected from atmospheric influences and the influences of the moon and sunlight; because of the sympathetic magnetic action of the earth in stimulating and developing the inner senses and the inner body; because of certain races who live in the interior of the earth and who may be met with in the recesses of the earth only; and because of means there available for rapid and safe transportation through the earth which cannot be had over the earth's surface. Such caves as are chosen are not mere holes in the ground. They are the gateways of avenues leading into grand courts, spacious halls, beautiful temples and vast spaces within the earth, awaiting those ready to enter them.

Forests are chosen by some adepts and masters on account of the activity of vegetable life and animal forms, and because their work may be with the life and types of animals and plants, and because the vegetable and animal forms are dealt with in the instruction of their disciples.

Mountains are the resorts of adepts, masters and mahatmas, not only because of their geographical positions, the seclusion which they afford, and because the air is lighter, purer and better suited to their bodies, but because from mountains certain forces can be best and most easily controlled and directed.

Deserts are sometimes preferred because they are free from demoniacal and inimical elementary presences and influences, and because the dangers attending travel over desert country will keep inquisitive and meddlesome people away, and because the sand or underlying strata afford magnetic and electric conditions necessary to their work, and generally because of climatic advantages. Great deserts are usually free from these elementary presences because great deserts have been ocean beds. Though these ocean beds may have been the scenes of human life before they became such, the atmosphere has been cleared and purified by the submerging of the land. When the waters of the ocean roll over a country they destroy not only the astral bodies of beings who have lived there, but they also disintegrate the elementaries; that is, inimical desire-bodies of human beings who have lived there. The old countries of Europe which have been above water for thousands of years, and have given birth to family after family of the old races, have hovering over the land the presences of many of the old heroes who have lived and fought and died and who persist about the earth in a thought body, nourished and perpetuated by the thought of the people. Pictures of the past are held in the atmosphere of such lands and are sometimes seen by those who put themselves in touch with the life of the past. Such presences often retard progress by holding the pictures of the past over the minds of the people. A desert is clear, and free from such influences.

Positions of importance on the earth, such as those where cities stood or stand, where rivers rolled or now flow, where volcanoes lie dormant or are active, and such places as are selected by adepts, masters and mahatmas as abodes are centers where invisible worlds and cosmic forces contact, enter or pass through or out of the earth. These points are physical centers which offer conditions under which cosmic influences may be more easily contacted.

Temples are built at important centers which are then used by adepts, masters and mahatmas for such purposes as the initiation of the inner bodies of their disciples into sympathetic relation with universal forces and elements, or the instruction of their disciples in the laws by which such forces, elements and bodies are controlled.

Adepts, masters and mahatmas may exist in their physical bodies in such places as outlined. They do not live in disorder and confusion. No master or mahatma would live with a people who persist in wrongdoing and who constantly act against law. No master or mahatma would live in the midst of discord or among impure physical bodies.

A few reasons have been given why adepts, masters and mahatmas select caves, forests, mountains and deserts as temporary or permanent abodes. It must not be supposed that every person who lives in a cave or a forest or on a mountain top or in a desert, is an adept, master or mahatma, though these places are adapted to their work. Those who seek to meet and know an adept, master or mahatma may go to caves, forests, mountains or deserts, and meet many people in each of these places, but will not know an adept, master or mahatma even if they stood before one, unless the seekers had some means of knowing him, aside from his physical appearance or from the location where they find him. One is not an adept because he lives in places removed from the habitations of men. Many strange looking human beings live in many of the places described, but they are not adepts, masters nor mahatmas. Living in a desert or on a mountain will not make a man a mahatma. Half breeds, mongrel types and degenerates of the races of men are found in those out of the way places. Men who are dissatisfied with or have a grudge against the world and their fellowmen have gone and go to lonely places and become hermits. Human beings with fanatical tendencies or religious mania have selected for themselves dismal and dangerous places to work off their fanaticism or give vent to their mania by doing penances through ceremonies or bodily torture. Introspective men have selected a waste country or deep forest as places of study. Yet none of these are adepts, masters or mahatmas. If we find men as natives or as old residents or as travellers, in desert or mountain, in forest or cave, and whether they be beetle-browed and uncouth or be handsome and polished in manner and speech, yet are neither their appearance and manners nor the place where they are found, indications that they are adepts, masters or mahatmas. Passing through a chemical laboratory one meets many students, but unless they are seen at their work and the instructions are heard which they receive he will not be able to distinguish between the students, assistants, professor or strangers, who may be present. In the same way one would hardly be able to distinguish an adept by his physical appearance or manner from others.

How can we know or meet an adept, master or mahatma, and would there be any advantage in such a meeting?

As has been indicated, an adept is a being distinct from his physical body; as an adept he lives and moves consciously, in the astral or psychic world. A master is a distinct being, aside from the physical body in which he lives, and as a master he thinks and acts in the mental world. A mahatma is a being quite different from his physical body, and as a mahatma he exists and knows and has his being in the spiritual world. Either of these beings may have and live in his physical body, but the physical body will give comparatively little evidence of who its inhabitant is.

To know an adept in the same manner as we know a physical body of a man, we must be able to enter the psychic world and there see the adept in his own world. The adept may make himself visible as an astral body and allow his body to be touched. Beings and creatures of the astral world have appeared in human form and subjected themselves to the senses of sight and touch in the physical world and have disappeared and faded away again even while being held by physical men, but those who held them were unable to tell anything except that they saw an appearance, touched it and saw it disappear. When a thing is brought from the invisible astral world into the physical world the man who is limited to his physical senses alone cannot understand the astral appearance except in physical terms, and none of the accompanying phenomena, if there be any, can be understood except in physical terms. Therefore, to know an astral creature or phenomenon or adept, one must be able to enter at will into or to look down upon the astral world. A master may look down upon, from the mental world and know anything in the astral world. An adept in the astral world may and will know another adept in that world; but an ordinary human being cannot really know an adept as an astral being because he has no such corresponding body as has the adept and therefore he cannot prove him. To enter and know the astral world from the physical, one must know in the physical those things and forces of the physical which correspond to the elements, forces or beings in the astral world. A medium enters the astral world, and frequently describes certain appearances, but the medium does not know about such appearances anything more than a child would know of differences and values of landscapes, or the materials used in painting.

The body or form of a master, as such, cannot be known by any of the physical senses, nor can it be known through, though it may be noticed by, the inner astral senses. A master does not deal directly with the forms of the astral world as does the adept. A master deals with thoughts chiefly; when desire is dealt with it is controlled or changed by him into thought. A master raises desire into thought and directs life by thought not merely as a human thinker would. A human thinker deals with life and changes desire into form by his thinking. But the human thinker is as a child in a kindergarten at play with building blocks when compared to a master, who would be as a builder capable of designing and directing the construction of edifices, mines, bridges and ships. The human thinker neither knows the material which he uses nor the essential nature, form or terms of existence of his thoughts. A master knows all this and, as a master, he deals consciously and intelligently with the life forces of the world and with the thoughts and ideals of men.

A mahatma body, as such, cannot be sensed by a physical man any more than a physical man is able to sense the presence of the ether of space; like the ether of space, the body of a mahatma requires finer faculties, of a mental and other than of a physical nature, to perceive it. A mahatma deals with the spiritual nature of man. Training men to think is a master's work, and instructing them in the transmutation of forms is an adept's work. A mahatma acts by knowledge in the spiritual world and deals with the minds of men when they are ready to learn of and enter the spiritual world and will live according to and by the laws of the spiritual world, in which all other manifested worlds are included.

It is useless, then, to guess that this or that person is or is not an adept, master or mahatma. It is folly to go on a mahatma hunt. It is foolish to believe that adepts, masters and mahatmas exist because some one in whom the believer has confidence says that this or that person is an adept, master or mahatma. No authority whatever outside of one's own knowledge is sufficient. If the existence of adepts, masters or mahatmas does not seem reasonable, after one has given the matter consideration and has thought of the problem without prejudice, then he is not to be blamed for not believing in them. No one should believe in their existence until life itself will present to him such facts and conditions as will allow him to say with reason that he feels and sees a necessity for the existence of such intelligences.

To accept adepts, masters or mahatmas on the authority of some one in whom we believe, and to grant as true that an adept, master or mahatma has said this or that, and to act on such suggestions and alleged commands unless they are reasonable, would be a return to the dark ages of ignorance and superstition and would encourage the setting up of a hierarchy by which the reason of man would be suppressed and he be subjected to fear and a condition of infantile life. Not by guessing, nor by wishing, nor by favor, but by an earnest and unselfish desire to know, an aspiration to the divine, by acting according to the knowledge of one's own better nature and the divine within him, and by a conscientious and unremitting endeavor to control one's lower by the better desires, and a careful, patient and continued effort to understand and control one's own thoughts, together with a feeling of the unity of life in all things, and with a sincere desire without hope of reward to gain knowledge, for the love of mankind: by these means one may come in contact with and prove and know, without harm to himself or others, of adepts, masters and mahatmas.

One is able to find an adept, or the adept will find him, when he has developed within himself somewhat of the nature of an adept, which is controlled desire. He is able to meet and prove a master as he is able to think and to live intelligently in the world of thought and when he himself has developed a body capable of living or thinking clearly in the thought or mental world. He will know a mahatma only when he has attained to a knowledge of his own individuality, knows himself to be I-am-I as distinguished from all other things.

Every one has the possibility of knowing adepts, masters and mahatmas; but it is a latent possibility, it is not actual ability. No one will ever be able to know an adept, master or mahatma, or to know the differences and relationships between them until he has at least apprehended these differences and relationships within his own make up. It is possible for a man to know these differences and to distinguish between the natures and beings within and outside himself even though he may not as yet have fully developed bodies equal to such beings.

By the inner senses, latent in most men, a man will find an adept. By his own power of thought and his ability to live in the thought or ideal mental world, a man may perceive and meet and prove a master. This he does by the thought body if he has developed one sufficiently. The thought body which each human being has is the body he uses when he dreams intelligently, in the dream world, while the physical body is asleep, and when his dreams are not caused by disturbance of the physical body. If one can act in his dream body consciously and when he is awake, he will be able to perceive and know and prove a master.

Every human being has a body of knowledge. This knowledge body is his individuality, which is not always evident to him because of the confusion caused in his mind by his senses and desires. By no other means than by his knowledge, apart from his thinking and his sensing, can man know a mahatma. Each man's knowledge body corresponds to and is in nature similar to the mahatma body.

Each human being senses directly or apprehends vaguely the different principles within himself which correspond to adept, master and mahatma bodies. The astral form body which holds the physical matter in form, linked with the desires which surge through his form body, is that by which a man will be able to tell an adept; but he will be able to tell to that degree only to which he is able to feel and sense his form body and direct the desires in it.

If he is unable to feel his own form body, and is unable to direct and control his own desires, he will not be able to tell whether or not a being is an adept, even though the investigator has objects precipitated from the astral world for him, or beings suddenly appear physically and disappear again, or he witnesses other strange phenomena. One will be able to meet or prove a master to be such when he is able to dream consciously and intelligently in his waking moments and while still conscious in his physical body.

One can be able, in his physical body, to know a mahatma as such, and distinct from other orders of intelligences, by his own knowledge body, which is in or through or above the physical. The knowledge body is that which intelligently persists in deep sleep, after the physical body with its desires and the formative body and the life thought body have been left behind. Then he, alone, as a knowledge body, exists in the spiritual world. All bodies and faculties are processes or degrees of becoming and attainment. The mahatma body is the attainment.

The physical body is the gross matter which contacts and acts in the physical world; the body which acts through the physical is the sense body or astral body, which senses the physical world and the elements and forces which act through it. The full and complete development of this sense body is adeptship. The life or thought body is that by which the forces and elements, their combinations through the physical, and their relationships are reasoned about. The thought body is distinctively human. It is the body of learning which is the result of numerous lives, in each of which are overcome forces of form and desire by one's increasing ability to think and to direct and control desires and forms by thought. The complete development and attainment is the thought body of a master. The knowledge body is that by which things are known. It is not the process of reasoning, which leads to knowledge, it is knowledge itself. That body of knowledge which is perfect and not obliged to go through reasoning processes and reincarnations is or corresponds to a mahatma body.

A man becomes an adept when he is able to move and act consciously in the astral world and deal with things in the astral world as he is capable of acting in his physical body in the physical world. Conscious entrance into the astral world is similar to a birth in the physical world, but the adept newly born into the astral world, though he is not at once fully equipped to deal with all things in the astral world, is yet able to move and live there, whereas the physical body of the human born into the physical world requires long care and growth before it can take care of itself in the physical world.

A man becomes a master when he knows the laws of his own life and has lived according to them and has completely controlled his desires and when he has entered and lives intelligently in the mental world and acts in the mental world in a mental body. The entrance of a man as a master into the mental world is like another birth. The entrance is made when he discovers or is aided in the discovery of himself as a mental body moving free in that mental world in which the mind of a thinking man now fumbles and moves laboriously in the dark.

A master becomes a mahatma when he has completely worked out all his karma, complied with all the laws demanding his presence in the physical, astral and mental worlds, and has done away with all necessity to reincarnate or appear in any of these. Then he enters the spiritual world and becomes immortal; that is to say, he has a body individual and immortal which will persist throughout the manifested and spiritual worlds so long as they shall last.

A man must become an adept, master or mahatma while his physical body is still alive. One does not become either, nor attain immortality, after death. After attaining adeptship, or becoming a master or mahatma, one may according to his class and degree remain away from the world or return to and act with the physical world. Adepts often work in the world though the world does not know them as adepts. Masters are rarely present in the busy world; only under most important circumstances do mahatmas move among the men of the world. Aside from any special mission which an adept, master or mahatma may undertake to the world, there are certain times when these intelligences do appear in and before the world and are known by men not, perhaps, by these terms or titles but by the work they do.

Their presence or appearance in the world is due to cyclic law brought about by the desires and thoughts and achievements of mankind, and when it is time to assist in the birth of a new race and the inauguration or re-establishment of a new old order of things. There is a cyclic law according to which adepts, masters and mahatmas appear successively to take part in the affairs of the world and as regularly as the coming of the seasons in their order.

Among the visible signs that an adept, master and mahatma has appeared, is here or will in the future appear, are the many people who claim to be adepts, masters or mahatmas. None of the claims, alleged messages, advices, proclamations, prove the passing, presence or coming of adepts, masters or mahatmas, but they do give evidence that the human heart yearns toward something and for the attainment of that something in man himself, which adepts, masters and mahatmas are. As the season of the year is announced by the passing of the sun into a particular sign of the zodiac, so the coming of an adept, master or mahatma is announced when the heart of humanity passes or reaches into the realms where adepts, masters and mahatmas dwell.

Besides the appearance of adepts, masters and mahatmas, due to the desires or aspirations of a people, these intelligences appear and give to the world at regular periods the results of the work done by them. When an adept, master or mahatma becomes such, then, in compliance with the law or of his own free will and for love of mankind, he comes into the world and makes a gift to the world of something which will show the path of travel which he has gone over, indicate dangers to be avoided, obstacles to be overcome, and work to be done. This is done that those following may be aided by their having gone on before. These gifts to the world are like sign-posts at cross roads, each indicating the road it is left to the traveller to choose.

When adepts, masters and mahatmas appear physically they do so in a body which will attract as little attention as the purpose for which they appear will allow. When they appear to a race it is usually in a physical body most suited to that race.

Adepts, masters and mahatmas carry on their work with the world in groups, each in turn being assisted in the general work by the others.

No part or section of the globe can do without the presence of an intelligence such as an adept, master or mahatma, any more than any department of government could continue without the guiding presence of its head. But as the heads of governments change, so change the presiding intelligences of a nation or race. The representative of government is an expression not of a few, but of the sum total of the will of the people. So is the intelligence presiding over nations and races. Adepts, masters and mahatmas are not like politicians who abuse, coddle or flatter the people and make promises, and so get themselves elected to office. Theirs is not a tyrannical tenure like that of many heads of governments. They do not try to outwit or break or make law. They are administrators of the law according to the demands in the hearts of the people, and they respond to them under the law of cycles.

(To be continued)

ADEPTS, MASTERS AND MAHATMAS

(Continued)

[From *The Word,* Vol. 10 No. 1, October 1909]

D UTY means more to adepts, masters and mahatmas than to ordinary mortals. Man's duty is important to him in proportion as he is sensible of his responsibilities to himself, to his family, his country, his humanity, to nature and to the divine principle in nature. These duties he performs or fails to perform in the short span of one life. The duties of adepts, masters and mahatmas lie in similar fields, but they see more than the mortal sees. Instead of being limited to mortal vision theirs is extended, according to their degree and attainment, up to an age of the world. The circle of duties of an adept includes the earth, and the elements and forces which surround and move through it, and which are the immediate causes of all physical changes and phenomena. The adept knows and deals with and wields forces and elements invisible to man. Like as the potter moulds his clay, so the adept shapes his material according to the purpose in view. His duties lie in producing phenomena, often strange to the senses of man, and in relating the material of the invisible world in which he lives and acts consciously, to the visible physical world of men. He needs and uses his physical body for his further development and in order to relate the invisible to the visible world.

The duties of adepts have caused some to be known to the world as magicians, though not all known as magicians are adepts. An adept renders service to the world at certain periods. Then he produces certain phenomena which are considered to be miracles by the ignorant and which the learned with limited vision declare impossible or impostures. An adept magician is one who produces phenomena according to natural laws unknown to the learned of the period. He may summon into visibility the presence of beings ordinarily invisible; he may command these presences to perform strange feats; he may cause storms to appear or disappear; he may bring about or quell conflagrations and floods, or bring about any natural phenomenon; he may levitate physical objects, produce music in the air without instruments, cause physical objects of little or great value to be precipitated from the air; he may cause the lame to walk; he may heal the sick or make the blind see, by speaking a few words or by the touch of his hand.

The adept magician renders service to the world when he does any of these phenomena, for the purpose of helping humanity and according to the law as directed by orders of intelligences higher than himself. But if he should produce phenomena from the sense of glorying in his power, from self-admiration and pride, or from any selfish motive, he will inevitably be punished by losing the power he has, incurring the censure of the higher orders of intelligence who act with the law, and a continuance of his actions will end in his ruin. Legend and ancient history give numerous examples of adept magicians.

What in one age seems improbable or impossible, becomes in a succeeding age natural and commonplace. To talk with a friend one mile or one thousand miles distant, would have been considered impossible one hundred years ago. The person claiming that such a thing was possible would have been considered a charlatan. It is now done daily. To illuminate a house by touching an electric button would then have been considered a magical performance. It excites little wonder to-day. If any one, twenty years ago, had said that it was possible to send wireless messages round the world he would have been considered as self-deceived or as a deliberate trickster who desired to attract attention. Since the telephone, electricity, and the Hertzian waves have been brought into common use, people to whom they were once wonders now regard them in a matter of fact way, and young people brought up to their use regard them with as little wonder as they do the growing of plants, the running of motor cars, the phenomena of sound or the mystery of light.

The adept magician works according to laws of the invisible world and produces results as certainly and definitely as the modern scientist who works according to known laws governing the physical world. It is no more difficult for an adept magician to precipitate a precious stone or other objects from the air, or to raise his body and be suspended in mid air, than it is for a chemist to precipitate oxygen and hydrogen as water by an electric spark, or to raise weights from the ground by the use of the magnet. The chemist precipitates the water by his knowledge of the elements, the electric spark unites them in certain proportions. The adept magician precipitates any object by knowledge of the constituents of the object in certain proportions, and by his ability to direct these constituents into the form held in his mind. The elements or constituents of all things which appear physically are held suspended in the atmosphere of the earth. The chemist or physicist may precipitate some of these into form by the means at hand and according to physical laws and by physical means. The adept magician is able to produce similar results without the limited physical means at the service of the physicist. The physicist uses a magnet to lift an iron bar. The adept magician uses a magnet which is not physical to lift his physical body, but his magnet is none the less a magnet. His magnet is his own invisible form body, which is the center of gravity for his physical body, and as his invisible body rises it acts as a magnet for his physical body which follows it. When the laws of the invisible world are understood they are no more and no less wonderful than the laws which govern the physical world and its phenomena.

Adepts may also take part in wars and in deciding the balance of power between nations, or they may appear as poets to appeal to the sentiments of mankind and to show through poetry the way nature works in her kingdoms and with the children of men. An adept may appear as a statesman endeavoring to shape the policy of a nation according to just laws in so far as the desires of the people will respond to such advices. In such duties as the adept assumes and whereby he takes part immediately in the affairs of mankind, he is working under the direction of masters who are wiser than he; he is the link between mankind and them; of course he is not known to be an adept, nor of any other order of men than those among whom he moves.

One who claims adeptship, whether by this or any like term, is either self-deceived or an impostor; or else, if he be an adept and makes the claim, he is either at once taken from his post or loses his caste and power and is no longer under the guidance of those masters who act according to just laws and for the good of the people. Initiation into any order higher than that of ordinary mankind prohibits such announcement by the one initiated. His claims become louder as his powers become weaker.

Masters do not come among men in their physical bodies as frequently as do adepts. Whereas the adept reaches and deals with men through his desires—his desires being of the physical world, it is necessary to contact men through the physical,—a master deals with men through his thoughts and according to his mental capacity and power, and it is therefore seldom necessary for a master to be among men in his physical body. The duties of a master as related to mankind are with the active mind of man. The mind of man acts on the plane of leo–sagittary (♌ – ♐), which is his mental world, and between virgo–scorpio (♍ – ♏) and libra (♎), which are the form–desire and the physical worlds below, and cancer–capricorn (♋ – ♑), which is the spiritual world above. The mind of man is attracted by the psychic and the physical worlds below and the spiritual world above or around. When an individual or a race is ready to receive instruction from a master or masters, the thoughts of the individual or race appear in the mental world, and according to the nature of the thoughts of such minds they receive instruction from a master. The minds receiving such instruction are at first not aware of the existence of masters, nor are they aware of receiving any instruction from any other order of beings or from any world except the world of the senses to which they are accustomed. A master holds out an ideal or ideals to an individual or a race and assists them in their mental operations in approaching or attaining their ideals, much the same as a teacher in a school sets examples and gives lessons to the scholars. and then aids the scholars in learning their lessons and in proving their examples. Masters encourage the efforts of an individual or the race in approaching their ideals, as good teachers encourage their scholars with the lessons. Masters do not force or carry the mind through the mental world, they show the way according to the capacity of the mind and its ability to travel. No master or set of masters would compel an individual or a race to continue his or its mental efforts if the individual or race did not choose to and would not go on with his or its efforts. When men choose to think and improve their minds, then they are assisted in their endeavors by masters according to the nature of their desires and aspirations.

The mind works its way through the mental world by its power to think. All minds capable of thinking enter the mental world and there learn as naturally and as orderly as the children of men enter and learn in the schools of men. As children are graded in their schools according to their mental fitness, so the minds of men are graded in the schools of the mental world according to their fitness. The schools of the mental world are conducted according to a just system of learning which is older than the world. The instruction in the schools of men will become similar to that of the schools of the mental world in proportion as the minds of men choose and act according to the just laws which prevail in the mental world.

Masters teach individuals and mankind as a whole through their thoughts and ideals in the particular grades of the mental world. Mankind is always being thus taught. The masters encourage and lead the races of mankind on and on, from one moral attainment to another through all stages and degrees of human progression, even though mankind be unconscious of the source from which it gets its inspiration to rise to higher levels. By one not limited, cramped and shut in by his range of vision in the span of one sensuous mortal life, it need not be considered strange that there should be schools in the mental world, nor that there should be masters, teachers, in the mental world, as there are human teachers in the schools of men. The mind is the teacher in the schools of men as it is in the schools of the mental world. Neither in the schools of men nor in the schools of the mental world can the teacher, the mind, be seen. Men learn and are educated concerning the things of the world of men in so far as the minds of men are capable of imparting information. No teacher in the schools of men can teach men the abstract problems of the mental world. These problems have to be battled with and mastered by the efforts of the individual minds. The problems of right and wrong, of human weal and woe, of misery and happiness, are worked out by the individual through his experience and efforts to understand and deal with these problems. A master is always ready to teach whenever men are ready to learn. In this way, in the mental world, mankind receives indirect teaching from the masters. Direct teaching from a master, as between teacher and pupil, is given when man has proven himself worthy to receive direct instruction.

A mahatma's duty to man is to bring him to an actual knowledge of what he, man, is as a spiritual being. Man represents an idea, a mahatma brings man to knowledge of the idea. Ideals are shown to men by masters who point the way to the ultimate idea from which ideals come. Mahatmas live in the spiritual world (♋ – ♑) and give the laws by which masters act. They are present at all times in the world but not in their physical bodies, therefore the world cannot know them.

Adepts, like men, have their likes and dislikes, because they work with desires and forms. An adept likes those who are of his kind and may dislike those who are opposed to him. His kind are those with whom he works. Those who are opposed to him are those of aims and desires other than his own, and who attempt to thwart him in his work. All adepts have their likes, but not all have dislikes. Those who have dislikes are adepts who seek power for themselves and who endeavor to subject others to their will. Adepts with good intent toward humanity have no dislikes for men. Masters are above dislikes, though they have their preferences. Their preferences are, like those of the adept, for those of their kind and for that for which they are working. A mahatma has no likes or dislikes.

The question of food, eating and drinking, has greatly troubled the minds of those who are striving for psychic faculties and alleged spiritual attainments. Food is a subject which should and does concern humanity. Food is of many kinds. Food is the material used in the building up and continuance of every kind of body. Food is a most important and difficult matter for humanity to agree upon, but there is no difficulty for the adept, master or mahatma in selecting and taking their nourishment.

Each kingdom of nature uses as food the one or more below it, and is itself as food to the kingdom above it. The elements are the food or material of which the earth is composed. The earth is the gross food from which plants are formed and grow. Plants are the material used as food for the building of an animal body. Animals, plants, earth and elements are all used as foods in the structure of the human body. The human body is that on which desire feeds and fattens. Desire is the material which is transformed into thought. Thought is food for the mind. Mind is the matter which makes the immortal individuality or perfect mind.

The adept selects the food which will give him a strong and healthy physical body. The kind of food which he selects for his physical body is largely determined by the conditions in which, or the people among whom, he is to work. He may eat meats and fruits, and vegetables and nuts and eggs and drink milk or water or the beverages of the time. He may eat or drink of each exclusively or partake of them all; but whatever foods he selects for his physical body will not be selected because of some fad but because he finds such food necessary for his physical body, through which he is to work. His physical body itself is really the food or material which he as an adept uses for the strengthening of himself as a desire form body. As his physical body is built from the essence of the foods which are taken into it, so he uses as food for his desire body the essences of his physical body. The food of an adept, as such, is not taken by eating and drinking, as the physical body takes its food. Instead of eating and drinking the adept renews, strengthens or continues himself as an adept by extracting or transforming the essences of his physical body into a magnetic body for himself as an adept.

The food of a master is not the food on which the physical body of a master subsists. The food of the physical body of a master is less earthy than the food of the physical body of an adept. A master sees that his physical body partakes of such food as is necessary for the maintenance of its health and soundness, though under certain conditions a master may sustain his physical body by the drinking of water and the breathing of pure air. A master uses his physical body for a higher purpose than does an adept. The body of the adept is his desire form, which is a magnetic body. The body of a master is his thought form, which is composed of pure life. A master does not transform or transfer the essences of the physical into the astral or desire body; a master transmutes desire into thought. A master raises the lower into higher desires and transmutes the desires, which are as food for thought. These thoughts are in turn the food or material of which the master or mental body is fashioned. A master, as such, does not eat and drink in order to persist, though he grows in power from or by thought.

The physical body of a mahatma requires less gross or earthy food than that of a master or an adept. The physical body of a mahatma does not depend for its continuance on solid foods. The food most necessary is the breathing of pure air. That is not the air breathed in by the physical man; it is the breath of life, which is the life of all bodies and which the physical body of the mahatma learns to breathe in and assimilate. The physical body of an adept is not able to make use of this breath of life which, even if breathed in, could not be held by the physical body. The physical body of a mahatma is of a higher order. Its nervous organization is magnetically balanced and capable of responding to and holding the electric current of life as it is breathed into the physical body of a mahatma. But the food for the mahatma, as such, is knowledge, which is spiritual.

Adepts, masters or mahatmas, as such, do not need physical clothes. Each body is the garment worn by the inner body, as clothes are garments for the physical body. The physical garments worn by their physical bodies are selected and used with respect to time, place and temperature and prevailing customs of the people among whom adepts, masters or mahatmas may move. Garments made of linen or wool or silk or fibres are worn according to the climate in which they are; skins of animals are also worn. In preparing the garment, a material is used which will afford protection for the body against the cold or heat or magnetic influence, or which will attract these influences. So the skin of an animal may protect the physical body from injurious magnetic influences from the earth. Silk will protect the body from electrical disturbances. Wool will attract some of the sun's rays in cold climates and conserve the heat of the body. Linen will reflect the heat of the sun and keep the body cool. Adepts, masters and mahatmas do not concern themselves about the clothing of their physical bodies as do the people of polite society and of refined tastes. Fashions in dress do not fill the minds of adepts, masters and mahatmas as they fill the minds of society people. The greater the intelligence, the more simple and plain his dress, if he selects it with respect to himself, though he will choose a costume suited to the people among whom he moves. A covering for the head, a garment for the body and protection for the feet, are all that he needs.

Amusements are arranged to attract and please the minds of children or give relaxation to those who have mental worry or overwork. Adepts, masters and mahatmas have no amusements though they have their recreation and pleasure. Recreation is given to their physical bodies, such as walking, climbing, or such gentle exercise as will keep the limbs and muscles of the physical body in condition. Their pleasure is in their work. The pleasure of an adept lies in seeing success attend his efforts to wield and mould the elements and the results attending what he does. A master's pleasure is found in seeing the improvement in the minds of men, in assisting them and in showing them how to control and direct their thoughts. The pleasure—if it can be called pleasure—of a mahatma is in his knowledge and power and seeing that law prevails.

All physical bodies, even those of adepts, masters and mahatmas, require sleep. No physical body of whatever kind or grade can exist without sleep. The time selected for sleep depends on the prevalence of the electric and magnetic currents of day and night, and of the breathing of the earth. The earth breathes in when the positive influence of the sun prevails; it breathes out when the positive influence from the moon prevails. The body is awake at the time when the positive electric influences of the sun are strongest. Sleep gives the best results to the body when the positive magnetic influence of the moon prevails. The positive electric influence of the sun is strongest when it crosses the meridian and at sunrise. The positive magnetic influence of the moon increases in strength from dark until after midnight. Sleep gives the time needed to remove the waste of the body and to repair the damage done by the work of the day. The sun sends currents of the electric force of life into the body. The moon sends streams of the magnetic force into the body. The electric influence from the sun is the life of the body. The magnetic influence from the moon forms the vehicle which holds and stores up the life from the sun. The invisible form body of man corresponds to and is of the nature of the magnetism from the moon. The influence from the sun is that which pulses through and keeps the body alive. As the life from the sun pours into the body it beats up against the invisible magnetic form body of the physical, and if this life current is kept up continuously it will break down and destroy the magnetic form body. While the mind is connected with and acts consciously through the physical body it attracts the solar life current to the body and prevents the lunar magnetic influence from acting naturally. Sleep is the withdrawal of the mind from the body and the turning on of the magnetic influence.

Adepts, masters and mahatmas know at what times of day or night it is best for their physical bodies to work and at what times to have rest. They can withdraw from the physical body at will, can prevent injurious influences from affecting it, and allow the magnetic influence to remove all wastes and repair all damages. Their physical bodies can have greater benefits in less time from sleep than those of ordinary men, because of their knowledge of the prevailing influences and of bodily needs.

The adept as such, apart from his physical body, does not require sleep in the sense in which the physical body does; nor is he unconscious during sleep, though there are periods when he rests and renews himself, which are analogous to sleep. Aside from his physical body, a master does not sleep in the sense of becoming unconscious. A master is conscious throughout an incarnation. But there is a period at the commencement of his incarnation when he passes into a state similar to that of dream, until he awakes as the master in his physical body. A mahatma is immortally conscious; that is to say, he maintains a continuous conscious existence through all changes and conditions throughout the entire period of evolution in which he acts, until he should some time decide to pass, or should at the end of the evolution pass, into that state known as nirvana.

(To be continued)

ADEPTS, MASTERS AND MAHATMAS

(Continued)

[From *The Word,* Vol. 10 No. 2, November 1909]

ADEPTS and masters are organized into lodges, schools, degrees, hierarchies and brotherhoods. A lodge is a dwelling place in which an adept, master or mahatma lives, or it is a place of meeting; the term school refers to the line or kind of work in which he is engaged; a degree shows his capacity, ability and efficiency in the work of his school; a hierarchy is the race to which he belongs; a brotherhood is the relationship which exists between those in lodges, schools and hierarchies. The organizations of adepts and masters are not like those of a theatrical company, a political party, or a stock corporation, which organizations are created by man-made laws. The organization of adepts and masters takes place according to natural laws and for purposes other than physical. The principle of organization is the relation of all parts of a body or order into one united whole for the benefit of the parts and the body as a whole.

The purpose of organization among adepts is to perfect their bodies, to direct desire and to control the forces of the unseen psychic world. They are organized in different schools according to degrees made up of many groups. Each group has a teacher; he selects, arranges and relates those whom he teaches into a harmonious, working body according to their natural qualities and capacities. He instructs the disciples in the use and control of their desires, in the control of elemental forces and invisible powers, and in producing natural phenomena by such control. As masters have not entirely worked out their karma, they are shown in their schools what that karma is and how best to work it out, how to perfect their thought or mental bodies, and what are the scope and mysteries of the mental world.

Mahatmas are not organized as are adepts and masters. Their physical bodies have little place in their organization, if such it can be called. They do not meet in groups or schools or hold conclaves for the purpose of instruction.

A hierarchy is sevenfold in its divisions. Seven races or hierarchies appear and are developed in their movable zodiac according to the laws of the permanent zodiac. (See "*The Word*," Vol. 4, Nos. 3–4 [*pp. 86–129 in* The Zodiac *in this book series*].) Each sign of the lower seven zodiacal signs represents a hierarchy, and each is distinct in its type and development from each of the other six hierarchies. The first hierarchy or race is of the sign cancer, breath, and belongs to the spiritual world. The second is of the sign leo, life, and belongs to the mental world. The third race or hierarchy is of the sign, virgo, form, and belongs to the psychic world. The fourth is of the sign libra, sex, and belongs to the physical world. The fifth is of the sign scorpio, desire, and belongs to the psychic world. The sixth is of the sign sagittary, thought, and belongs to the mental world. The seventh race or hierarchy is of the sign capricorn, individuality, and belongs to the spiritual world.

The first race of humanity were bodies of nascent minds, individual spiritual breaths. The second were electrical bodies of life force. The third were astral bodies. The fourth race were and are physical bodies, men, in and through whom the three previous races act as the form, the life, and the breath of the physical men.

All physical human beings now living and distinct in sex, of whatever country, clime or so-called race, are fourth race beings or bodies and are types of the fourth hierarchy. The different subraces, types and colors into which this fourth race is divided, are so many divisions of the hierarchy which are different in degree of development, but not in kind. In kind they are all physical human. Within and through the fourth race, the fifth race or hierarchy began to act and develop many thousands of years ago. This fifth race acting through the fourth race, which is the physical body, cannot be seen by fourth race men any more than fourth race, physical men can see the third or second or first races which are in and work through them. The fifth race acts through the physical race as desire, and although it cannot be seen by physical humanity, none the less it directs and compels physical humanity to its dictates. Fourth race or physical humanity has reached its lowest state of development as far as figure and substantiality are concerned; in future races the physical fourth race will be improved in beauty of figure, grace of movement, lustre of skin, color and strength and refinement of features, in proportion as the future races of humanity will act in and through it. The fifth hierarchy is made up of those beings who have developed through fourth race physical man, even as the fourth race were the outcome and development from the third race. The fifth race of humanity is the hierarchy here called adepts, who have been described as beings able to live apart and distinct from their fourth race physical bodies. The sixth race of humanity are the beings here called masters. The sixth race of humanity are mental bodies of thought which act on and direct, or should direct, fifth race desire, as fifth race desire impels fourth race physical men to action. The seventh hierarchy is the hierarchy herein called mahatmas. It is they, the most advanced, who are guides, rulers and law givers of all the races of humanity.

Physical fourth race man has acting in him desire, the fifth race or hierarchy, which he is trying to develop. The sixth race acts through physical fourth race man as his thinker. The seventh race acts through fourth race physical man as his I-am-I principle, or that in him which is direct and instant knowledge. The desire principle and thinking principle and knowing principle now present in the fourth race physical man are the fifth, sixth and seventh races of humanity herein called adepts, masters and mahatmas. They are now principles only; they will be developed into beings who will become consciously and intelligently active in the psychic, mental and spiritual worlds in which adepts, masters and mahatmas now act fully conscious and intelligent.

A brotherhood is the common relationship between those of any one or of all the hierarchies. Brothers of physical humanity are those who have physical bodies. They are fourth race brothers. Brotherhood among the race of adepts exists not because of physical relationship but because they are fifth race brothers. Likeness of the nature and object of desire are the bonds of special brotherhoods among adepts. The bond of brotherhood among the masters is thought. They are sixth race brothers. Sameness of ideals or subjects of thought determine the divisions of the brotherhood. A master enters another division of his hierarchy when the subjects of his thoughts and ideals become the same as those of that other. What he is, links a mahatma with his seventh race brothers.

Besides the brotherhoods in each of the hierarchies, there is the brotherhood of humanity. It exists in each of the worlds and in every hierarchy. The brotherhood of humanity is made up of those in every race who think and act for humanity as a whole rather than for any group or degree or school or hierarchy.

As to the subject of government: The distinctness of desire, the power of thought, and the knowledge, which adepts and masters have, prevent in their government the confusion resulting from the prejudices, beliefs and opinions among men in blind attempts at self-government, if not from selfish rule. The government of adepts and masters is decided by the nature and fitness of the bodies and intelligences who make up the government. There is no placing in office by trickery, mob violence, or arbitrary appointment. Those who govern become governors by their growth and development into the office. Those who are governed or advised receive such advice readily, because they know that decisions and advice are given justly.

Adepts and masters, as such, do not live in cities or communities. But there are communities where adepts and masters live in their physical bodies. Conveniences are had which are necessary for eating and drinking and taking care of their physical bodies. There is at least one community which is made up of the physical bodies of adepts, masters and mahatmas and a certain primitive, physical race of beings who are representatives of the early fourth race stock of humanity. This early fourth race began its existence in the middle of the third race. These primitive beings are not the Todas mentioned by H. P. Blavatsky in Isis Unveiled, and they are not known to the world. These families have been preserved in their early purity. They are not addicted to the degraded practices and indulgences which the physical race of humanity now spreads over the entire earth.

It would be unreasonable to suppose that adepts, masters and mahatmas in their physical bodies are free from all manner of dangers, diseases and changes. These are present throughout the manifested worlds, though in one world they are not the same as in the other worlds. Each world has its preventatives, antidotes, remedies, or cures, to protect the bodies of its world from the dangers, diseases and changes to which they are subject. It is left to each intelligent being to decide what his course of action shall be and to act freely according to what he decides.

Adepts, masters and mahatmas, as such, are not subject to the dangers, diseases and changes to which their physical bodies are subject. Their physical bodies are physical and mortal, are under the laws governing physical matter, and are subject to the dangers, diseases and changes to which all other mortal fourth race physical bodies are subject. The physical bodies of adepts, masters and mahatmas may be burned by fire, drowned, or crushed by rocks. Their physical bodies will contract diseases affecting other mortal human bodies if subjected to the conditions for such diseases. These bodies feel heat and cold and have the same senses as other human bodies; they pass through the changes of youth and age and as physical bodies they die when the span of physical life has ended.

But because the physical bodies of adepts, masters and mahatmas are subject to the same dangers, diseases and changes to which mortal man is heir, it does not follow that they allow their physical bodies to incur any of the effects resulting from the dangers, diseases and changes from which the human mortal man suffers, except the change known as physical death.

Physical man rushes into danger, breathes disease and meets death because he is ignorant of what he does; or if not ignorant, because he is unable to restrain and control his appetites, desires and longings for things and conditions which cause disease and hasten death.

In walking over a dangerous country any man is likely to be injured or killed, but one in possession of his senses is less likely to suffer injuries than he who attempts the journey and is blind. The ordinary man of the physical world is blind to the effects of his appetites and desires and deaf to his reason. Hence the misfortunes and disease attending in his journey through life. If an adept, master or mahatma walked off a precipice in his physical body and allowed his physical body to fall, it would be killed. But he knows when and where there is danger and avoids or protects himself against it. He does not allow the physical body to suffer disease because he knows the laws of health and makes the physical body conform to them.

An adept, master or mahatma may do with his physical body that which would cause injury or death to an ordinary man. A master might, in his physical body, move among lions, tigers and venomous reptiles without harm to his body. He does not fear them, and they do not fear him. He has conquered the principle of desire in himself, which is the actuating principle in all animal bodies. Animals recognize his power and are unable to act against it. Their desire is powerless to injure him. This is so, not because they could not crush and tear and chew or sting his physical body, as physical matter, but because his physical body is not moved by sex desire and therefore not by hate or fear or anger, which move other physical bodies and which excite the fear or hatred or anger of animals; so animals do not attempt to injure, any more than they attempt to scratch water or crush the air. Because of his knowledge of natural laws and his ability to transmute matter, the adept can avert disasters impending from earthquakes, storms, fires or volcanic eruptions; also the effects of poisons can be overcome by him with antidotes, or by causing the organs of the body to liberate secretions in quantities necessary to overcome and equalize the poison.

Although an adept is not subject to diseases and death as is his physical body, yet as a being of desire in form he is liable to incur injuries and changes which are of a psychic nature. As an adept, he cannot suffer, in any physical sense, from falls or fire, nor can he be injured by wild beasts nor affected by poisons. Although he does not suffer from things which are physical, yet he may be subject to what in the astral world is analogous to these things. He may be affected by envy which will act in him as a poison unless he eradicates and overcomes it or uses a virtue to counteract its effect. He may be torn by rage, anger or hatred, if he will not subdue these evils, as by wild beasts. Although he cannot fall, failure to overcome vices will lower him in degree and in power in his world. He may be borne down by pride as by a storm, and burned by fire of his own desires.

As a master is a being of the mental world he is not subject to the afflictions which spring from desire, nor is he subject to any dangers, ills and changes of the physical world. The thoughts and ideals with which he has worked and by which he has become a master may in turn be checks to his progress and powers, by which he may be injured if he does not overcome or grow out of them as he overcame desire. Because of his overcoming desire as a blind force and as the root of appetites and of attraction to sensual forms, by the power of his thought, thought may assume for him an importance beyond its real value, and by thought a master may build a mental wall about himself which will shut out the light from the spiritual world. If he attaches overmuch value to thought he becomes cold and removed from the physical world and thinks alone with himself in his own mental world.

A mahatma is not subject to any of the dangers, ills or limitations prevailing in the physical or psychic or mental worlds, in any sense which these terms imply. Yet he may be affected by his very knowledge resulting from his great degree of attainment. He is immortal and not subject to the changes of the lower worlds; desire as such has no part in him; he is beyond the requirements of thought and the processes of thinking; he is knowledge. He knows his power, and the idea of power is so strong in him that there may develop from it egoism or egotism. Egoism carried to the extreme results in his seeing himself as God through all the worlds. Egotism ultimately results in being conscious of I as the only I or being. The power of egotism may be so great as to cut off all the worlds and then he is conscious of nothing else but himself.

Throughout the manifested worlds there are two things which are with humanity through all its transformations and attainments. They follow and inevitably conquer each unit of humanity unless such unit conquers and uses them. These two things are by man called time and space.

Time is the change of the ultimate particles of matter in their relationship to each other, as matter flows through the worlds in its coming and going. Matter is dual. Matter is spirit-matter. Matter is materialized spirit. Spirit is spiritualized matter. Space is the sameness in the one. In this sameness are continued the manifested worlds and in it the operations of time are performed. Failure to conquer time results in death in that world in which the individual unit of humanity is acting. Difference in time in the different worlds is difference in the changes of the matter of each of these worlds. Time is overcome in any of the worlds when one strikes a balance between the opposites in the spirit-matter in that world. When one strikes the balance between the particles of time or matter, the change of matter, time, stops for him. When change ceases, time is conquered. But if time is not conquered when the balance should be struck then the change called death takes place, and man departs from the world in which he has been acting and retreats to another world. As time is not conquered in the world of retreat, death again conquers. So the individual unit passes from the physical body through the psychic and often to its heaven world, but always back again to the physical world, constantly confronted by time and overtaken by death, which forces it from world to world if he has failed to strike the balance in time.

An adept is he who has balanced between physical matter and balanced between form matter and balanced between desire matter. He has arrested the change in physical matter by conquering it and is consciously born into the desire world. Change goes on in the matter of his desire world, and at the time for the balancing the matter of his desire world he must balance it or death will overtake and drive him from the desire world. If he strikes the balance and stops the change in his desire matter he will overcome desire and the death in the desire world and be born consciously into the thought world. He is then a master, and as a master he meets and deals with the matter, or time, of the mental world and must there too balance and arrest the time of the mental world. Should he fail, death, the high officer of time, takes him from the mental world and he returns to begin again with the physical time matter. Should he balance the matter of the mental world and arrest thought he overcomes change in the thought world and is born a mahatma into the spiritual world. The overcoming of desire, the conquering of the changes of thought and of the matter of the mental world, is immortality.

There is still change in the spiritual world of knowledge. The immortal is an individual unit of humanity who has asserted and attained his individuality in the spiritual world and has knowledge of the changes in the lower worlds of time matter. But the change which he has yet to conquer is the change in spiritual immortal matter; he overcomes it by striking the balance between his own immortal self and all other units of humanity in whichever world they may be. If he fails to strike the balance between himself and the other spiritual units of humanity he is under the spell of the death of separateness. This death of separateness is extreme egotism. Then this high spiritual being has reached the limit of attainment so far as the unit of humanity is concerned and he will remain in his state of egotism, conscious, knowing of himself only, throughout the entire period of manifestation of the spiritual world.

Sameness is in the time matter of the physical world and in the time matter of each of the other worlds. The ability to balance the opposites in matter depends upon seeing sameness as it is through the changes of matter and to relate the matter to sameness, not to see sameness as matter. Failure to recognize sameness through the operations of time results in ignorance. Failing or unwilling to see the sameness of space through physical matter, a man cannot balance the physical sex matter, cannot arrest the changes in the desire matter, cannot equilibrate nor stay the thought matter, and the mortal cannot become an immortal.

There are two types of adepts, masters and mahatmas: those who act for themselves, separately and selfishly, and those who act for humanity as a whole.

An individual unit of humanity may attain to immortality as a mahatma in the spiritual world of knowledge by beginning in the physical world to balance sex matter even without perceiving sameness through the matter. He begins by seeing matter as sameness rather than sameness through matter. A balance is thus struck, but not a true balance. This is ignorance and results from not learning to see the true, distinct from the appearance. As he continues through the worlds, mistaking matter for sameness, his ignorance concerning the true and the impermanent continues from world to world. Selfishness and separateness inevitably are with man as long as he does not truly balance the matter of each world. When sameness, space, is not mastered but man goes on, ignorance is with him from world to world, and in the spiritual world he has knowledge, but without wisdom. Knowledge without wisdom acts selfishly and with the idea of being separate. The result is the nirvana of annihilation at the end of the manifestation of the worlds. When sameness is seen and the idea mastered and acted on, then time as change of matter is balanced in all the worlds, death is conquered, space is conquered, selfishness and separateness disappear and the one thus knowing, sees that he, as an individual immortal unit of humanity, is in no way separate from any of the other units in any of the manifested worlds. He is wise. He has wisdom. Such a one puts knowledge to the best use for all beings. Knowing of the relationship existing between all humanity he wisely decides to assist all other units and worlds according to the laws governing the worlds. He is a mahatma who is a guide and ruler of humanity and one of the brotherhood of humanity before mentioned.

A mahatma may decide to keep a body, the form body of the physical, in which he can communicate with and be seen by humanity. Then he overcomes in his physical body time and death in the physical world by immortalizing the form of the physical body, not physical matter as such. He puts the body through a course of training and provides it with particular foods which he gradually diminishes in quantity. The body increases in strength and gradually throws off its physical particles, but maintains its form. This continues until all the physical particles have been thrown off and the body of form stands, the conqueror of death, in the physical world, where it may be seen by men, though it lives in the form–desire world and is known as an adept, an adept of a higher order. This body is the one which has been spoken of in theosophical teachings as nirmanakaya.

That class of mahatmas in whom egotism is developed leave the psychic and the mental bodies, which they have developed, continue in their spiritual body of knowledge and shut themselves out from all things of the world; they enjoy the bliss which comes from the attainment and knowledge of self and the power that attends it. They have during their incarnations sought immortality and bliss for themselves alone, and having attained immortality they have no care for the world or their fellows in it. They have worked for the overcoming of matter; they have overcome matter, and have a right to the rewards resulting from their work. So they enjoy that selfish bliss and become oblivious of all outside themselves. Although they have overcome matter, time, they have conquered it only for one period of its manifestations. Not having mastered sameness, space, in which time moves, they are still under the dominion of space.

Those mahatmas who do not shut out the world remain in touch with the world of men by keeping their mental thought body, in which case they contact the minds only of men and are not seen or known by men through their senses. The same method of developing this immortal body of physical form is used by both types of mahatmas.

The mahatma who develops his physical form body can appear to men in the physical world in the form of man, a flame of fire, a pillar of light, or as a globe of splendor. The purpose of a mahatma who remains in contact with the world is to govern a race of men or mankind as a whole, to control the minds of men, to direct their action, prescribe laws and to have the worship and adoration of mankind. This purpose is the outcome of the development of egoism carried to its extreme. The power which they have and their knowledge enable them to carry out their purpose. When one becomes a mahatma of this type, in whom egoism is fully developed, he naturally perceives his own godship. He is a god and wills that his power and knowledge shall rule the worlds and men. On becoming such a mahatma he may establish a new religion in the world. The greater number of the world's religions are the result of and have been brought into being and established by a mahatma of this kind.

When such a mahatma wills to rule men and have them obey him he looks into their minds and selects among mankind that mind which he sees is best fitted to be his instrument for establishing a new religion. When the man is chosen, he guides him and prepares him and often causes him to apprehend that he is being guided by a superior power. If the mahatma is one who has a mental thought body only, he entrances the man of his selection and lifts him into the mental world, which is his heaven world, and there instructs him that he, the man, is to be the founder of a new religion and his, God's, representative on earth. He then gives instructions to the man so entranced as to the manner of founding the religion. The man returns to his body and relates the instruction received. If the mahatma has developed and uses the form body it is not necessary for him to entrance the one whom he has selected as his representative among men. The mahatma may appear to him and entrust him with his mission while the man is in possession of his physical senses. Whichever course the mahatma pursues, the man selected believes that he is the one among all men who is favored by God, the one and only God. This belief gives him a zeal and power which nothing else can give. In this condition he receives guidance from his acknowledged god and proceeds with superhuman efforts to do the will of his god. People feeling a power about the man gather around him, share in his zeal, and come under the influence and power of the new god. The mahatma gives to his mouthpiece laws, rules, rituals and admonitions for his worshippers, who receive them as divine laws.

Worshippers of such gods confidently believe that their god is the true and only God. The manner and method of his revelation, and the worship which he exacts, show the character of the God.

This should be judged not by wild fancies or orgies, nor by the bigotry and fanaticism of later followers and their theology, but by the laws and teachings given during the life-time of the founder of the religion. Religions are necessary to certain groups of races, who are as sheep needing a fold and a shepherd. The mahatma or god gives a certain protection to his followers and often guides and sheds a beneficent and protective influence over his people. A religion represents one of the schools in which mankind is taught while the mind is in its youthful stages of development.

There are other forces and beings, however, which are neither friendly nor indifferent to man but who are inimical and evilly disposed to human-kind. Among such beings are some adepts. They, too, appear to man. When they give him some revelation and empower him to start a religion or society or form a group of men in which pernicious teachings are imparted, diabolical practices observed, and lewd and licentious ceremonies are held which require the shedding of blood and gruesome, ghoulish and disgusting indulgences. These cults are not restricted to one locality; they are in every part of the world. At first, they are known to few, but if secretly desired or tolerated, a religion based on such practices will appear and grow as it finds room in the hearts of people. The old world and its people is honeycombed with such cults. Hordes of human beings hurl themselves madly into the vortices of such cults and are consumed.

Man should not fear to believe in one or many gods and their creeds, but he should be careful in entrusting himself to a religion, teaching or god, who requires unreasoning faith with absolute devotion. There comes a time in the life of each when religions no longer teach him, but merely show the record of what he has passed through and has outgrown. There comes a time when he passes from the infant class of humanity into a state of responsibility in which he must choose for himself not only concerning the things of the world and a code of morals, but concerning his belief in a divinity inside himself and outside.

(To be continued)

———————————

ADEPTS, MASTERS AND MAHATMAS

(Continued)

[From *The Word,* Vol. 10 No. 3, December 1909]

AMONG those who have heard of and desired to become adepts, masters and mahatmas, many have busied themselves, not with preparation, but have tried to be one right away. So they have arranged with some alleged teacher to give them instruction. If such aspirants had used better sense they would see that if adepts, masters and mahatmas do exist, and are possessed of wonderful powers and have wisdom, they have no time to gratify the whims of such foolish persons by teaching them tricks, exhibiting powers, and holding court for the simple minded.

There are many obstacles in the way of those desiring to become disciples. Ungoverned anger, passion, appetites and desires, will disqualify an aspirant; so will a virulent or wasting disease, such as cancer or consumption, or a disease preventing the natural action of internal organs, such as gall stones, goitre and paralysis; so will amputation of a limb, or loss of the use of an organ of sense, such as the eye, because the organs are necessary to the disciple as they are the centers of forces through which the disciple is instructed.

One who is addicted to the use of intoxicating liquors disqualifies himself by such use, because alcohol is an enemy to the mind. The spirit of alcohol is not of our evolution. It is of a different evolution. It is an enemy of the mind. The internal use of alcohol impairs the health of the body, overstimulates the nerves, unbalances the mind or ousts it from its seat in and control of the body.

Mediums and those who frequent seance rooms are not fit subjects for discipleship, because they have around them the shadows or ghosts of the dead. A medium attracts into its atmosphere creatures of the night, those of the sepulchre and charnel house, who seek a human body for the things of the flesh—which they have lost or never had. While such creatures are the companions of man he is unfit to be a disciple of any adept or master who is a friend of humanity. A medium loses the conscious use of his faculties and senses while his body is obsessed. A disciple must have the full use of his faculties and senses and possess and control his own body. Hence somnambulists and those suffering from dementia, that is, any abnormal action or unsoundness of mind, are unfitted. The body of the somnambulist acts without the presence and direction of the mind and is therefore not to be trusted. No one who is subject to hypnotic influence is fit for discipleship, because he comes too easily under the influence which he should control. The confirmed christian scientist is unfit and useless as a disciple, because a disciple must have an open mind and an understanding ready to accept truths, whereas the christian scientist closes his mind to certain truths which his theories oppose and compels his mind to accept as true, assertions which outrage sense and reason.

From the human standpoint, the schools of adepts and masters may be divided into two kinds: the school of the senses and the school of the mind. In both schools the mind is, of course, that which is instructed, but in the school of the senses the mind of the disciple is instructed in the development and use of the senses. In the school of the senses the disciples are instructed in the development of their psychic faculties, such as clairvoyance and clairaudience, in the development of the psychic or desire body and how to live apart from the physical and act in the desire world; whereas in the school of the mind, the disciple is instructed in the use and development of his mind and of the faculties of the mind, such as thought transference and imagination, the faculty of image building, and in the development of a thought body able to live and act freely in the world of thought. Adepts are the teachers in the school of the senses; masters are the teachers in the school of the mind.

It is most important that an aspirant for discipleship should understand the distinction between these two schools, before he becomes more than an aspirant. If he understands the difference before becoming a disciple he may save himself long lives of suffering and harm. The majority of aspirants, though not knowing the differences between adepts, masters and mahatmas (or other terms which are used synonymously or in connection with these names), earnestly desire psychic powers and the development of a psychic body in which they can ramble around in the now invisible world. Though unconsciously to them, this longing and desire is in the school of the adepts an application for admission. Acceptance of the application and admission to the school of the adepts is, as in the schools of men, announced to the applicant when he proves himself fit for admission. He proves himself not by formally answering questions as to what he has learned and what he is prepared to learn, but by having certain psychic senses and faculties.

Those desiring to be disciples, whose efforts are to think clearly and understand definitely what they think, who take delight in following an idea through processes of thought as it is reflected in the world of thought, who see the expression of thoughts in their physical forms, who trace the forms of things back through processes of thought to the idea from which they originate, those who endeavor to understand the causes which actuate human emotions and control human destinies, are those who have made or are making their application for admission to discipleship in the school of the masters. Their acceptance as disciples is known to them as soon as they have developed mental faculties which fit them for and make them ready to receive instruction in the school of the masters.

Aspirants for discipleship are generally more attracted by those things which appeal to the senses than by that which appeals to the mind, hence many enter the school of the senses as compared to few who enter the school of the mind. The aspirant should decide which school he will enter. He may select either. His choice followed by his work, will determine his future. At the initial stage, he may decide clearly and without difficulty. After his choice is made and his life is given to his choice, it is difficult or nearly impossible for him to retract his choice. Those who choose the school of the masters may, on becoming a master, become a mahatma and then only, safely become an adept. Those who choose and enter the school of the senses, and who become adepts, seldom if ever become masters or mahatmas. The reason is that if they have not seen and understood the difference between the mind and the senses, or if they have seen the difference and then have selected and entered the school of the senses, then, after entering it and developing the senses and body used in that school, they will be too much concerned with and overwhelmed by the senses to be able to free themselves and rise above them; for after developing that body which overcomes the death of the physical, the mind adjusts itself to and works in that body, and it is then usually unable to act independently of and apart from it. This condition may be understood in ordinary life. In youth the mind may be exercised and cultivated and engage in the pursuit of literature, mathematics, chemistry or another of the sciences. The mind may have disliked or rebelled against such work, but the work becomes easier as it goes on. As age advances, intellectual power increases and at an advanced age the mind is able to enjoy literature or the sciences. On the other hand, a man under similar circumstances and at the outset even more favorably disposed to mental work, may have been led away from it if he has followed a life of pleasure. Living for the day only, he is less and less inclined to take up any serious study. As age advances, he finds it impossible to follow a mathematical or any process of reasoning and he is unable to comprehend the principles of any science. He might feel attracted to some intellectual pursuit but withdraws at the thought of beginning it.

The mind of one who has chosen and entered the school of the senses, and has overcome physical death and has become an adept, is like the mind of one immersed in pleasures and unused to abstract thinking. He finds himself incapable to begin the task because the bent of his mind prevents it. Regrets may haunt him for lost or discarded opportunities, but with no avail. The pleasures of the physical are many, but the pleasures and attractions of the psychic world are a thousandfold more numerous, alluring and intense for one who has become enchanted by them. He becomes drunk with the use of astral faculties and powers, even though there be moments, as in the case of the sufferer from alcohol, when he wishes to escape their influence; but he cannot free himself. The world-old tragedy of the moth and the flame is again enacted.

No adept or master would accept as a disciple one who did not have a reasonably sound mind in a reasonably sound body. A sound and clean mind in a sound and clean body are requisites to discipleship. A sensible person should comply with these requisites before trusting himself to be a disciple and receive instruction directly or indirectly from an adept or a master.

One should study well his motive in wishing to be a disciple. If his motive is not prompted by the love of service to his fellow men, as much as for his own advancement, it will be better for him to postpone his attempt until such time as he can feel himself in the hearts of others and feel mankind in his own heart.

If the aspirant decides for discipleship he becomes by such decision, a self appointed disciple in the school of his selection. There is no school or body of men to whom the self appointed disciple should apply and make known his wishes. He may enter into so called secret societies or occult or esoteric bodies or join people claiming acquaintance with adepts, masters or mahatmas or giving instruction on the occult sciences; and though there may be a society here and there, perhaps, who may be able to give some little instruction in obscure matters, yet by professing or insinuating intimacy with adepts, masters or mahatmas, they are, by their very claims and insinuations, self-condemned and show that they have no such relation or connection.

The self appointed disciple is the only witness of his appointment. No other witness is needed. If a self appointed disciple is of the stuff of which true disciples are made, he will feel that so-called documentary evidence will be of little or no importance in deciding a matter in which lives of effort are concerned.

One who wishes assurances that he will be admitted to some school, he who is doubtful as to whether there is or is not a school, and he who feels that in becoming a disciple he must receive recognition soon after wishing to be a disciple, such as these are not yet ready to be self appointed disciples. Such as these fail before they have fairly begun the task. They lose confidence in themselves or in the reality of their quest, and, when tossed about by the stern realities of life, or when intoxicated by the allurements of the senses, they forget their determination or laugh at themselves that they could have made it. Such thoughts and many more of a similar nature arise in the mind of the self appointed disciple. But he who is of the right stuff is not swerved out of his course. Such thoughts, the understanding and dispersing of them, are among the means by which he proves himself. The self appointed disciple who will eventually become an entered disciple, knows that he has set himself a task which may take many lives of unremitting effort, and although he may often feel discouraged at his seemingly slow progress in self preparation, yet his determination is fixed and he steers his course accordingly. The self preparation of the self appointed disciple in the school of the senses is parallel or similar to that in the school of the mind, for a considerable time; that is, both endeavor to control their appetites, direct their thoughts to the studies at hand, eliminate customs and habits which distract them from their self appointed work, and both fix their minds on their ideals.

Food is a subject about which the aspirant is concerned at an early stage, very often the would-be aspirant never gets any further than the subject of food. There are notions about food among faddists who are fasters or vegetable or other "arians." If the aspirant flounders on the food rock he will be stranded there for the remainder of his incarnation. The aspirant is in no danger from food when he sees and understands that a strong and healthy body, not food, is that with which he is most concerned. He will value and take such foods as will keep his body in health and increase his strength. By observation and, perhaps, by a little personal experience, the aspirant sees that fasters, vegetarians and fruitarians, are often fussy, irritable and ill-tempered people, gross or wizened in person, that unless they have had trained minds before they became vegetarians they are unable to think long or consecutively on any problem; that they are flabby and fanciful in thought and ideal. At best they are weak minds in bulky bodies, or keen minds in weak bodies. He will see that they are not strong and healthy minds in strong and healthy bodies. The aspirant must begin or continue from where he is, not from some point in the future. It is not impossible to live an ordinary life and preserve health without the use of meat for some singularly constituted bodies. But in the present physical body of man, he is constituted an herbivorous and a carnivorous animal. He has a stomach which is a meat eating organ. Two thirds of his teeth are carnivorous teeth. These are among the unfailing signs that nature has provided the mind with a carnivorous body, which requires meat as well as fruits or vegetables to keep it in health and preserve its strength. No amount of sentimentality nor theories of any kind will overcome such facts.

There does come a time, when the disciple is nearing adeptship or mastership, when he discontinues the use of meat and may not use solid or liquid food of any kind; but he does not give up the use of meat while he is actively engaged in large cities and with other men. He may discard the use of meat before he is ready, but he pays the penalty by a weakly and sickly body, or by a fidgety, ill-tempered, irritable or unbalanced mind.

One of the chief reasons advanced for the giving up of meat is, that the eating of it increases the animal desires in man. It is also said that man must kill out his desires to become spiritual. The eating of meat does strengthen the animal body in man, which is of desire. But if man did not need an animal body he would not have a physical body, which is a natural animal. Without an animal body, and a strong animal body, the aspirant will not be able to travel the course mapped out for himself. His animal body is the beast which he has in keeping, and by the training of which he will prove himself ready for further progress. His animal body is the beast which he is to ride and guide over the course he has chosen. If he kills it or weakens it by refusing it the food which it needs, before he has well set out on his journey, he will not get far on the road. The self appointed disciple should not attempt to kill or weaken desire, the beast in his keeping; he should care for and have as strong an animal as he can, that he may complete his journey. His business is to control the animal and compel it to carry him where he wills. It is not true, as often claimed, that the meat which man eats is filled with the desires of the animal, or has fanciful, astral desires hanging around it. Any clean meat is as free from such desires as a clean potato or a handful of peas. The animal and its desires leave the meat as soon as the blood is out of it. A clean piece of meat is one of the most highly developed foods that man may eat and the kind of food which is most easily transferred to the tissues of his body. Some of the races may be able to preserve health without the use of meat, but they may do it by reason of climate and by generations of hereditary training. Western races are meat eating races.

The self appointed disciple in the school of the senses and also in the school of the mind, requires strong desire, and his desire must be to attain his object, which is conscious and intelligent discipleship. He must not run away from things which seem obstacles on his path; he must walk through and overcome them fearlessly. No weakling can succeed. It requires a strong desire and a fixed determination to undertake and make the journey. One who supposes that he must wait until conditions are ready for him, one who thinks that things will be done for him by unseen powers, had better not begin. He who believes that his position in life, his circumstances, family, relationships, age and encumbrances, are obstacles too great to overcome, is correct. His belief proves that he does not understand the work before him and that he is, therefore, not ready to begin. When he has a strong desire, a firm conviction in the reality of his quest, and has the determination to go on, he is ready to begin. He does begin: from that point. He is a self appointed disciple.

A man may appoint himself a disciple in either of the schools, no matter how poor or rich he may be, no matter how deficient in or possessed of "education," no matter whether he is a slave of conditions, or in what part of the world he is. He may be a dweller of the sun-baked deserts or the snow-clad hills, of broad green fields or of crowded cities; his post might be on a lightship out at sea or in the bedlam of the stock exchange. Wherever he is, there he may appoint himself disciple.

Age or other bodily limitations may prevent him from becoming an entered disciple in one of the lodges of either of the schools, but no such conditions can prevent him from being a self appointed disciple in his present life. If one so wills, the present life is the one in which he becomes a self appointed disciple.

Obstacles beset the self appointed disciple at every turn. He must not run away from them, nor ignore them. He must stand his ground and deal with them according to his ability. No obstacle or combination of obstacles can overcome him—if he does not give up the fight. Each obstacle overcome gives an added power which enables him to overcome the next. Each victory won brings him nearer to success. He learns how to think by thinking; he learns how to act by acting. Whether he is aware of it or not, every obstacle, every trial, every sorrow, temptation, trouble or care is not where it is to be the cause of lamentations, but to teach him how to think and how to act. Whatever the difficulty he has to contend with, it is there to teach him something; to develop him in some way. Until that difficulty is met properly, it will remain. When he has met the difficulty and has dealt with it squarely and learned what it had for him, it will disappear. It may hold him for a long time or it may disappear like magic. The length of its stay or the quickness of its removal depends on his treatment of it. From the time it begins to dawn on the self appointed disciple that all his troubles, difficulties and woes, as well as his pleasures and pastimes, have a definite place in his education and character, he begins to live confidently and without fear. He is now preparing himself to be a duly entered disciple.

As a man about to begin a long journey takes with him only what is necessary on the journey and leaves other things behind, so a self appointed disciple attaches himself to that only which is necessary to his work and leaves other things alone. This does not mean that he ceases to care for the things valuable to him alone; he must value a thing for what it is worth to others as well as for what it is worth to him. What is more important to him than conditions, environment and position, is the manner in which he meets, thinks and acts with these. As a day is made up of hours, the hours of minutes, the minutes of seconds, so his life is made up of greater and lesser events, and these of trivial affairs. If the aspirant manages the unseen little affairs of life thoroughly, and intelligently controls unimportant events, these will show him how to act and decide the important events. The great events of life are like public performances. Each actor learns or fails to learn his part. All this he does unseen by the public eye, but what he does in public is what he has learned to do in private. Like the secret workings of nature, the aspirant must work unceasingly and in darkness before he will see the results of his work. Years or lives may be spent in which he may see little progress, yet he must not cease working. Like a seed planted in the ground, he must work in darkness before he can see the clear light. The aspirant need not rush out into the world to do any important work in order to prepare himself; he need not race over the world in order to learn; he himself is the subject of his study; he himself is the thing to be overcome; he himself is the material which he works with; he himself is the result of his efforts; and he will see in time what he has done, by what he is.

The aspirant should check outbursts of anger and passion. Anger, passion and fits of temper are volcanic in their action, they disrupt his body and waste his nervous force. Inordinate appetite for foods or pleasures must be subdued. The body or bodily appetites should be gratified when they are necessary to bodily health.

The physical body should be studied; it should be cared for patiently, not abused. The body should be made to feel that it is the friend, instead of the enemy, of the aspirant. When this is done and the physical body feels that it is being cared for and protected, things may be done with it which were impossible before. It will reveal more to the aspirant concerning its anatomy, physiology and chemistry, than may be learned of these sciences at a university. The body will be a friend to the aspirant, but it is an unreasoning animal and must be checked, controlled and directed. Like the animal, it rebels whenever control is attempted, but respects and is the willing servant of its master.

Natural pleasures and exercises should be taken, not indulged in. Health of mind and body are what the aspirant should seek. Harmless outdoor pleasures and exercises such as swimming, boating, walking, moderate climbing, are good for the body. Close observation of the earth, its structure and the lives it contains, of the water and of the things in it, of the trees and what they support, of clouds, landscapes and natural phenomena, as well as study of the habits of insects, birds and fishes, will afford pleasure to the mind of the aspirant. All these have a special meaning for him and he may learn from them what the books fail to teach.

If a self appointed disciple is a medium he must overcome his mediumistic tendencies, else he will surely fail in his quest. Neither of the schools will accept a medium as disciple. By a medium is meant one who loses conscious control of his body at any time other than that of normal sleep. A medium is the tool for unprogressed, disembodied human desires and for other entities, particularly for inimical forces or the sprites of nature, the desire of which is to experience sensation and make sport of a human body. It is twaddle to speak about the necessity of mediums for receiving instruction from high spiritual intelligences beyond man. A high intelligence will no more seek a medium as his mouthpiece than a home government would select a blithering idiot as messenger to one of its colonies. When the higher intelligences wish to communicate with man they find no difficulty in giving their message to mankind through a channel which is intelligent, and by means which will not deprive the messenger of his manhood nor cause the pitiful or disgusting spectacle which a medium is.

An aspirant who is mediumistic may overcome his tendencies. But to do so he must act firmly and decisively. He cannot parley with or be lenient to his mediumism. He must stop it with all the force of his will. Mediumistic tendencies in an aspirant will surely disappear and cease altogether if he sets his mind firmly against them and refuses to allow any such tendency to become manifest. If he is able to do this he will feel an increase in power and an improvement of mind.

The aspirant must not allow money or the possession of it to be an attraction to him. If he feels that he is wealthy and has power and is of importance because he has much money and power, or if he feels poor and of no account because he has little or none, his belief will prevent further progress. The aspirant's wealth or poverty is in his power of thought and in faculties other than those of the physical world, not in money. The aspirant, if he is poor, will have enough for his needs; he will have no more, no matter what his possessions may be, if he is a true aspirant.

A self appointed disciple should not affiliate with any set of people to whose method of belief or form of faith he must subscribe, if these are different from his own or if they limit in any way the free action and use of his mind. He may express his own beliefs, but he must not insist on the acceptance of these by any person or set of persons. He must in no sense attempt to control the free action or thought of anyone, even as he would not wish others to control him. No aspirant nor disciple is at all able to control another before he can control himself. His efforts at self-control will give him so much work and require so much attention as to prevent him from attempting the control of another. The self appointed disciple may not in his life become an accepted disciple in either of the schools, but he should continue to the end of life, if his belief is real to him. He should be prepared to be made aware at any time of his acceptance as disciple, and prepared to continue many lives without acceptance.

The self appointed disciple who will be accepted in the school of the senses, the adepts, whether his choice has been made clearly and distinctly to himself or because of an ill-defined motive and natural bent, will be more interested in psychic faculties and their development than in processes of thought concerning the causes of existence. He will concern himself with the psychic world and will endeavor to enter it. He will seek to gain entrance into the astral by the development of his psychic faculties, such as clairvoyance or clairaudience. He may try one or many of the methods which are recommended by different teachers on the subject, discarding the unfit and using such as are suited to his nature and motive, or he may try new methods and observances which he will himself discover as he continues to ponder over the object of his desire, that is, his conscious existence apart from the physical body and the using and enjoying of the faculties attending such existence. The oftener he changes methods or systems the longer it will be before he obtains results. To get results he should hold to some one system and continue with that until he either gets proper results or proves the system to be wrong. Evidence that any system is wrong is not that results do not come quickly nor even after long practice, but such evidence may be found in this: that the system is either contrary to the experience of his senses, or is illogical and against his reason. He shall not change his system or method of practice merely because somebody has said so or because he has read something in a book, but only if what he has so heard or read is quite apparent or demonstrable to his senses, and self-evident to his understanding. The sooner he insists on himself judging the matter by his own sensing or by his own reasoning, the sooner will he outgrow the class of aspirants and the sooner will he enter as disciple.

As he continues his practice, his senses become keener. His dreams at night may be more vivid. Faces or figures may appear before his inner eye; scenes of unfamiliar places may pass before him. These will be either in the open space or appear like a picture in a frame; they will not be like a painted portrait or landscape. The trees and clouds and water will be as trees and clouds and water are. The faces or figures will be like faces or figures and not like portraits. Sound as music and noise may be heard. If music is sensed there will be no disharmonies in it. When music is sensed it seems to come from everywhere or nowhere. After it is sensed the ear is then no longer enraptured by instrumental music. Instrumental music is like the straining or snapping of strings, the clanging of bells or the shrill blowing of whistles. Instrumental music is at best the harsh imitation or reflection of the music of sound in space.

Nearby or approaching beings or objects may be felt without moving the physical body. But such feeling will not be as is the touching of a cup or of a stone. It will be of a lightness as of a breath, which when first experienced plays gently over or through the body which it contacts. A being or object thus felt will be sensed in its nature and not by physical touch.

Foods and other objects may be tasted without physical contact. They may be familiar or strange in taste; the taste will not be experienced in the tongue specifically but rather in the glands of the throat, and thence through the fluids of the body. Odors will be sensed which will be different from the fragrance coming from a flower. It will be as of an essence which seems to penetrate, surround and lift the body and produce a sense of exaltation of body.

The self appointed disciple may experience any or all of these new senses, which are the astral duplicates of the physical senses. This sensing of the new world is by no means an entrance into and living in the astral world. This sensing of a new world is often mistaken for entrance into it. Such mistake is a proof that the one who senses is not fit to be trusted in the new world. The astral world is new as well to the one who first senses it as to the one who, after long years of sensing, supposes that he has entered it.

Clairvoyants and clairaudients and the like do not act intelligently when they see or hear. They are like babes in a wonder world. They do not know how to translate correctly the thing they see, into what it is, nor do they know what is meant by what they hear. They think that they go out into the world but they do not leave their body, (unless they are mediums, in which case they are personally unconscious).

The new senses which are thus beginning to function are an evidence to the self appointed disciple that he is forging ahead in his efforts of self development. Until he has more evidence than the use of the senses here outlined, he should not make the mistake and suppose that he is acting intelligently in the astral world, nor should he suppose that he is yet a fully accepted disciple. When he is an accepted disciple he will have better evidence of it than that of clairvoyance or clairaudience. He should not believe what apparitions or unseen voices may tell him, but he should question all he sees and hears if it seems worth while, and if not, he should command what he sees to disappear, or bid the unseen voice be still. He should stop using such faculties if he finds himself passing into a trance or becoming unconscious, as a medium would, while using them. He should never forget that mediumship debars him from obtaining admission into the school of the adepts or of the masters, and that if a medium he can never become an adept or a master.

The self appointed disciple should understand that he should not indulge in the use of his new senses for pleasure to himself or for exhibitions of any kind which will afford amusement to others or win for him their approbation or applause. If desire for approbation by exhibiting the new senses or by informing others of his developing new senses is present in his mind, he will lose them partially or entirely. This loss is for his good. If he is on the right path they will not appear again until he has overcome his desire to be admired. If he is to be of use in the world he must work without desire of praise; if at the outset he desires praise, this desire will increase with his powers and would render him incapable of recognizing and remedying mistakes.

The self appointed disciple who has thus advanced and who, whether he made few or many mistakes, has been conscious of and corrected his mistakes, will at some time have a new experience. His senses will seem to melt into each other and he will find himself not so much in a place as in a condition, in which he will be aware that he is an accepted disciple. This experience will not be like that of a trance, in which he becomes partially or wholly unconscious, and after which he forgets in part or entirely what has occurred. He will remember all that there occurred and will not have been unconscious concerning any of it. This experience will be as the beginning and living of a new life. It means that he has found and duly entered as a disciple into the school of his selection, which is the school of the senses. This experience does not mean that he is yet able to live apart from his physical body. It means that he has entered the school in which he is to be taught how to live apart from and independent of his physical body. When he has learned so to live and act independently of his physical body he will be an adept.

This new experience is the beginning of his term of discipleship. In it he will see who or what his teacher is, and be aware of certain other disciples with whom he will be connected and instructed by the teacher. This new experience will pass from him,

who before was a self appointed but who is now an accepted disciple. Yet the experience will live with him. By it his teacher will
have imparted to the disciple a new sense, by which he will be able
to test the other senses and the correctness of the evidence which
they may furnish him. This new sense by which the teacher communicates with his disciple is the sense by which he as aspirant became disciple. His fellow disciples may never have been known to
him, but by the new sense he will learn who they are and meet
them, and they will be and are his brothers. These others form
with himself a set or class of disciples which will be instructed by
their teacher. His teacher will be an adept or an advanced disciple.
His fellow disciples may be living in other parts of the world, or in
his immediate neighborhood. If they are far removed from each
other, their conditions, affairs and circumstances in life will
change so that they will be brought near to each other. Until each
disciple is adjusted to his fellow disciples he will be instructed
when necessary by his teacher. When the disciples are ready to be
instructed as a class they are called together in their physical bodies
by their teacher, and are formed into a regular class of disciples and
taught by the teacher in his physical body.

The teaching is not from books, though books may be used in
connection with the teaching. The teaching deals with the elements and forces; how they affect the new sense or senses acquired; how to control them by the senses; how the physical body
is to be trained and used in the work. No member of this set of
disciples is allowed to make the existence of his class known to the
world, or to anyone not a disciple or not connected with his class.
Every disciple worthy of the name, of any school, avoids notoriety.
A disciple would usually suffer death rather than make his class

known to the world. Anyone professing to be a disciple and to receive instruction from any adept or master is not the kind of disciple here spoken of. He belongs to one of the so-called occult or secret societies which profess secrecy, but which lose no opportunity to advertise themselves to the world.

A self appointed disciple takes or makes for himself a set of rules by which he tries to live. An accepted disciple has placed before him a set of rules, which he must observe and put into practice. Among these rules are some concerning the physical body, and others for the development and birth of a new body as adept. Among the rules applying to the physical body are: observance of the laws of one's country, of relation to family, of chastity, of care and treatment of body, non-interference by others with his body. Among the rules applying to the body of the new psychic faculties are those concerning obedience, mediumship, disputes or arguments, treatment of desires, treatment of other disciples, use of senses and powers.

As to the rules for the body. The rules require that a disciple shall not violate the laws of the country in which he lives. In relation to family, the disciple shall fulfil his duties to parents, wife and children. If a separation from wife or children should take place it shall be upon the request and act of wife or children; separation must not be provoked by the disciple. As to chastity, if the disciple is unmarried, at the time of becoming disciple he shall remain unmarried providing that by so doing he will maintain his chastity, but if he cannot remain chaste in desire and act then he should marry. As regards the married state. The rule concerning chastity requires that the disciple shall not incite his wife's desire and that he shall earnestly endeavor to control his own. The rule concerning chastity forbids the use of the sex function under any pretext whatever, except for natural relationship between man and woman. As to care and treatment of body, it is required that that food shall be eaten which is best for the health and strength of the body, and that the body shall be kept clean, nourished and cared for, and be given the exercise, rest and sleep found necessary to the maintenance of bodily health. All alcoholic stimulants and drugs producing an unconscious state are to be avoided. The rule relating to non-interference by others with his body, means that the disciple should under no circumstances or pretence allow anyone to mesmerise or hypnotise him.

Among the rules concerning the development of the psychic body and its faculties, is that of obedience. Obedience means that the disciple shall implicitly obey the orders of his teacher in all that concerns the development of the psychic body and its faculties; that he shall observe strict allegiance in desire and thought to the school of his selection; that he shall continue to work for this school throughout the period of the gestation of his psychic body, no matter how many lives this may require, until birth as an adept. The rule concerning mediumship requires the disciple to use every precaution against himself becoming a medium and that he will not aid, nor encourage others to become mediums. The rule relating to disputes and arguments requires that the disciple shall not dispute or argue with his fellow disciples nor with other men. Disputes and arguments breed ill-feeling, quarrels and anger and must be suppressed. All matters relating to their studies, when not understood between themselves, should be referred by the disciples to their teacher. If not then agreed on, the matter shall be left alone until their growing faculties will have mastered it. Agreement and understanding of the subject will come, but not by argument or dispute, which confuse rather than make clear. As regards others, the disciple may state his views if he wishes, but must cease argument if he feels antagonism rising within himself. The rule concerning the treatment of desires requires that he shall cultivate and nourish that which is known as desire in so far as he is able to contain it within himself and to control its expression, and that he shall have one firm fixed and unrelenting desire for attaining birth as an adept. The rule regarding the treatment of other disciples requires that the disciples shall regard them nearer than his blood relatives; that he shall willingly sacrifice himself or any of his possessions or powers to assist a brother disciple, if by such sacrifice he does not take from or interfere with his family or act against the laws of the country in which he lives, and if such sacrifice is not forbidden by his teacher. Should a disciple feel anger or jealousy he must search out its source and transmute it. He interferes with his own and the progress of his class by allowing any ill-feeling toward his fellow disciples to exist. The rule applying to the treatment of senses and powers is, that they should be regarded as means to an end, the end being full adeptship; that they shall not be used to attract attention, to gratify the desire of any person, to influence others, to defeat enemies, to protect oneself, or to come into contact with or control the forces and elements, except as directed by the teacher. The disciple is forbidden to make any attempt to project himself out of his physical body, or leave his physical body, or aid another disciple to do so. Any such attempt, whatever the temptation, may be followed by a miscarriage in the birth of the disciple's new body and may result in insanity and death. Such miscarriage will prevent him from coming to birth in his present life and will cause tendencies to mediumship or to a like miscarriage in a succeeding life.

The duties of a disciple in his relation to the world are provided for by the karma of his past lives and are those which are naturally presented to him. A disciple lives inside of his life in the world. As he lives a more interior life, he may wish to leave the world of men and live with those of the school to which he belongs. Such desire is however forbidden and must be subdued by the disciple, as desire to leave the world will result in his leaving it, but there remains the necessity to return again until he can work in the world without the desire to leave it. The disciple's work in the world may cover a series of lives, but there comes a time when it is either necessary for him to leave it for a short or long time or altogether. This time is determined by the completion of duties to relatives and friends, and by the growth and development of the new psychic body to be born at the end of discipleship.

(To be continued)

ADEPTS, MASTERS AND MAHATMAS

(Continued)

[From *The Word,* Vol. 10 No. 4, January 1910]

THERE are many grades through which the disciple passes before he becomes an adept. He may have one or more teachers. During this period he is instructed in the natural phenomena which are the subjects of the outer sciences, such as the structure and formation of the earth, of plants, of the water and its distribution, and of the biology and chemistry in relation to these. In addition to and in connection with this, he is taught the inner sciences of earth, water, air and fire. He is shown and learns how fire is the origin and mover of all things which come into manifestation; how in its aspects it is the cause of change in all bodies and how by the changes caused by it, it receives all manifested things back into itself. The disciple is shown and sees how air is the medium and neutral state through which unmanifested fire causes the immaterial things to be prepared and made ready to pass into manifestation; how those things about to pass out of manifestation, pass into the air and are suspended in air; how air is the medium between the senses and the mind, between things which apply to the physical and those which appeal to the mind. Water is shown to be the receiver of all things and forms from the air and to be the fashioner and transmitter of these to the earth; to be the giver of physical life, and to be the cleanser and remodeller and equalizer and distributor of life to the world. Earth is shown to be the field in which matter is equilibrated and balanced in its involutions and evolutions, the field in which fire, air and water meet and are related.

The disciple is shown the servants and workers of and in these different elements, with the forces acting through them, though he is not as disciple brought into the presence of the rulers of the elements. He sees how fire, air, water and earth are the fields of action of the four races or hierarchies which are mentioned. How the three races preceding the physical body are of the fire, air and water. He meets the bodies belonging to these races and sees their relation to his own physical body, that of earth which is composed of beings belonging to these races. Besides these four elements, he is shown the fifth, in which he will be born as an adept at the completion of his development. The disciple is instructed concerning these races, their powers and action, but he is not carried into the realms or spheres of these races until he is more than a disciple. Some beings of these races are summoned before his developing senses that he may become familiar with them before birth among them and before he is trusted and allowed to act independently in and among them.

The disciple is instructed concerning the earth and its inner side; he may even be taken in his physical body to some interior parts of the earth, where he will meet some of the races spoken of. The disciple is taught concerning the magnetic qualities of minerals and is shown how the magnetic power acts in and through the earth and his own physical body. He is shown how magnetism as a body and a force acts within himself and how the body may be repaired in its structure and strengthened as a reservoir of life. Among the duties required of him may be that he shall learn the power of healing by magnetism and to make of himself a fit reservoir and transmitter of life. The disciple is instructed in the qualities of plants; he is shown how forms of life are developed through them; he is taught the seasons and cycles of the action of the sap of plants, of their potencies and essences; he is shown how to compound and manipulate these essences as simples, drugs or poisons, and the action of these on the tissues of human and other bodies. He is shown how poisons become antidotes to poison, how antidotes are administered and what is the law of proportion controlling these.

It may be required of him in his duties in the world that he be a prominent or an obscure physician. As such, he may impart the information to self appointed disciples who are fit to receive it, or he may give to the world such information as it can use to advantage.

The disciple is instructed concerning the astral remains of dead men; that is to say, the remains of the cast off desires of those who have died. He is shown how the desires last for a long or a short time and are remodelled and adjusted to the ego coming again into physical life. The disciple is shown desire forms, their different natures and powers and how they act on the physical world. He is shown harmless and inimical creatures who live in the atmosphere of man. It may be required of him to prevent such beings from attacking mankind, when mankind allows of protection. It may also be his duty to disintegrate some of these beings when they pass beyond their boundaries and interfere with man. But the disciple cannot suppress such creatures if the desires and thoughts of men will not permit. He is taught the means of communicating with and summoning the presence of beings of these worlds; that is to say, he is instructed, in their names, the forms of their names, the pronunciation and intonation of these names, and the symbols and seals which stand for and compel them. He must become thoroughly familiar with these matters under the immediate supervision of his teacher, before he is allowed to practice alone. If the disciple attempts to command these presences or influences without having thoroughly mastered them, he may lose his life in a similar manner as one who loses it while experimenting with chemistry or electricity, without due precautions to protect himself.

The disciple who in that life is to be born into the new life as adept, is before his turn of life required to leave the busy life of men and retire to some quiet and secluded place or to a community of the school to which he belongs. The turn of life of man is the beginning of the decline of his physical power. With some men this happens at thirty-five and with others not until their fiftieth year. The rise of life of physical manhood is marked by the increase of power of the seminal principle. This power increases until it reaches its highest point, then it begins to decrease in strength until man may become as impotent as he was in the child state. The turn of life comes after the highest point of seminal power. The disciple cannot always tell when the highest point is reached; but if he leaves the world for the purpose of adeptship in that life and body, it must be while his power is increasing and not when it is in its decline. The sex function must have ceased in thought and act before he can begin the forming of that body the birth of which will make of him an adept. When he leaves the world for this purpose he breaks no relationships, neglects no trusts, is not serenaded and his departure is not announced. He often leaves unnoticed and his mission is unknown to men. His departure is as natural as the passing of an hour.

The disciple now comes under the care and direction of the experienced adept who is to be present with him till birth. The disciple passes through a process analogous to that through which woman passes during the gestation and birth of a child. All seminal wastes are stopped, the forces and essences of the body conserved as taught him in his initial stages of discipleship. He is shown how each individual organ of the body gives up something of itself toward the formation and development of the body which is being formed through, as much as within him; though that which is being formed in the new body is not of the same kind nor for the same purpose as the organ from which it comes. Full adepts as such, in and out of physical bodies, are now met and communicated with by the disciple, as he progresses in his development toward adeptship. This is so, that he may become more and more familiar with the nature and life of an adept and in order that he may intelligently come to birth. He may live among or visit a community of adepts or one in which adepts rule.

In a community such as before described as that of the early race of physical man who are preserved in their natural purity, the disciple sees physical humanity as they were before the class of sensual minds had incarnated among them. This stock was preserved in order that mankind might be carried in its physical line unbroken from the time of the inception of the physical until the time of its passing from fourth race physical humanity into fifth race and sixth race and seventh race humanity, or through physical, psychic, mental and spiritual stages; humans, adepts, masters and mahatmas. The pure physical race among whom the adepts move are seen by the disciple to have a season ordained by nature for self reproduction. He sees that they have no desire for sex apart from such seasons. He sees in them the types of strength and beauty, and grace of motion into which the present humanity is destined to grow again when they shall have learned to grow out of and beyond their present appetites of sex and sense. This community of early humanity regard the adepts and masters who may be among them, as children regard their fathers; in simplicity and candor, but without the fear or apprehensions which some children have of their parents. The disciple learns that if a disciple should fail during the period through which he now passes, he is not lost nor entangled or retarded by after death states before returning into life as other men may be, but that he who fails to attain adeptship after he has reached a certain point along the path of attainment, is guided by the adept under whose direction he acts through the after death states and back into physical life and birth as one of the community among whom the adepts live. In that birth he will surely attain adeptship.

As the disciple advances he sees that adepts, as such, do not have internal organs similar to those in their physical bodies. He sees that the organs of the physical body are required for the generation and preservation of the physical body, but besides that they correspond to powers and faculties of other worlds. The alimentary canal is not needed in the adept because the adept as such requires no physical food. There is not secretion of bile nor circulation of blood in the adept, nor are there any of the products manufactured and elaborated by the physical body to maintain its structure. The adept has his physical body which does all this, but he is a separate being and is not his physical body. True, the physical of the adept has its virgo form body (♍ linga sharira), but the astral adept body here spoken of is the perfected adept body, the scorpio desire body (♏ kama), which is the complement of the virgo form body.

The disciple senses the changes going on within and through his physical body and is made aware of his approaching birth. This is the event of his lives of effort. His birth is equal to a physical death. It is a separation of body from body. It may be preceded by a conflux and tumult of the forces and fluids of the physical body and attended by apprehension or by calm and mellowness like as of the evening, at the glowing of the setting sun. Whether his travail be like unto the rumbling thunder amid the deepening darkness of gathering clouds or the quiet glory of the dying sun, the seeming death of the physical is followed by birth. As after a storm or luminous sunset the darkness is brightened by the stars and the light flood of the rising moon, so emerges out of the effort of overcoming, so grows out of death, the new born being. The adept emerges from or through his physical body into that world which he seemed to know so well but which he finds he knew but little. His adept teacher, present at his birth, adjusts him to the world in which he now lives. Like the changes in the infant's body which are effected by its entrance into the physical world, so changes take place in the new born adept as he rises from his physical body. But unlike the infant, he is in possession of his new senses and is not helpless.

Much of that which has been described of the life of the aspirant in the school of the senses applies to the self appointed disciple in the school of the masters, in so far as it pertains to the observance of self-control and care of body. But the requirements of the aspirant for discipleship in the school of the masters differ from those of the other school in that the self appointed disciple shall not attempt the development or use of the psychic senses. He must use his physical senses in the observation of facts and in the recording of experiences, but must accept nothing as proved to him by his senses unless it is sanctioned by his mind. His senses bear evidence, but the test of these is made by reason. There is no age limit for the aspirant to discipleship in the school of the masters. One may appoint himself a disciple when very old. He may not become an accepted and entered disciple in that life, but his step will bring him nearer to the point of discipleship in a succeeding life. The self appointed disciple is usually one concerning himself with obscure things, asking himself or others questions not generally thought about. He may be interested in subjects of mystery to the senses or in mental problems and processes. Psychic faculties may have been possessed by him from birth or they make their appearance during the course of his studies. In either case, the self appointed disciple who wants to enter the school of the masters must suppress and stop the use of these faculties. Suppression without injury is had by turning his interest from the senses themselves to the subjects which these senses present. The self appointed disciple who is in natural possession of psychic faculties can make rapid progress in mental development if he will close the doors to the psychic world. When he so shuts the doors he should try to gain entrance to the mental world by using and developing the mental faculties. When he dams the psychic floods they rise as energy and he receives an accretion of mental power. This path may take a long time to travel as compared with the results gained in the school of the senses, but in the end it is the shortest way to immortality.

(To be continued)

ADEPTS, MASTERS AND MAHATMAS

(Continued)

[From *The Word,* Vol. 10 No. 5, February 1910]

IN turning the mind from the senses to the subjects which the senses represent, one may clearly distinguish the difference between the school of the adepts, and the school of the masters. The school of the adepts controls or attempts to control the mind and senses by means of the senses. The school of the masters controls the mind and the senses by faculties of the mind. To attempt to control the mind by means of the senses is like harnessing and attempting to drive a horse with its head to the wagon. If the driver makes the horse go forward, then he goes backward; if he drives the horse backward then he will go forward but will never reach his journey's end. If, after thus teaching his horse and learning to drive it, he should reverse the process, his progress will be slow, because he must not only learn himself and teach the horse the proper way, but both must unlearn what had been learned. The time spent in becoming an adept is the time used in learning to drive the horse backward. After a disciple has become an adept and learned to drive the mind by means of the senses, it is almost impossible for him to take the better way of directing the senses by means of the mind.

The disciple self appointed to the school of the masters turns his study from the senses and the objects of the senses to the subjects of which these objects are the reflections. The subjects of what is received through the senses as objects, are perceived as subjects by turning the thought from the senses to that which they reflect. In doing this the aspirant is selecting for his discipleship the school of the mind; yet he does not forsake the senses. He must learn in them and through them. When he experiences through the senses, then his thought, instead of dwelling on the experience, reverts to what the experience teaches. As he learns what the experience teaches he turns his thought to the necessity of the senses for the experience of the mind. Then he may think concerning the causes of existence. Thinking of the causes of existence makes the disciple, who is self appointed to the school of the masters, adjust and relate the senses to the mind, lets him distinguish the differences between the mind and the senses and lets him see the modes of action of each. The aspirant to discipleship in the school of the masters will have experiences similar to those of the disciple self appointed to the school of the senses. But instead of attempting to draw the mind into and unite the mind with the senses, as by dwelling on a dream, looking at an astral figure or landscape and trying to continue to see and experience them, he asks and finds out what the dream means and what caused it and to what subjects the figure or landscape refer and what they are. By so doing he sharpens his thinking faculty, checks the opening of psychic faculties, lessens the power of the senses in their influence on the mind, separates in thought the mind from the senses, and learns that if the mind will not work for the senses the senses must work for the mind. In this way he becomes more confident and his thought acts more freely and more independently of the senses. He may continue to dream, but the subjects of which he dreams are considered instead of the dream; he may cease to dream, but the subjects of dreams will then take the place of the dreams and be present in his thought as dreams were to his astral vision. His thought is referred to the subjects of his senses instead of to the objects which the senses seek. Should the psychic senses manifest themselves, then that which they produce is treated similarly to what is observed through the physical senses. The aspirant learns to regard his senses as imperfect mirrors; that which they make manifest, as reflections. As when seeing a reflection in a mirror he would turn to the thing which it reflects, so in looking at an object his thought turns to the subject of which it is the reflection. Through sight he sees the object, but his thought rests not on the object except as on a reflection. He seeks the meaning of the object and its cause; and these may be found in the mental world, as thoughts; and beyond the thoughts, as ideas.

If the aspirant finds the meaning and cause of any object of the senses, he will instead of valuing the object for what it appears to be and the sense which tells him what it is, consider his sense as a mirror only whether it be an imperfect or a true mirror, and the object as an imperfect or true reflection only. Therefore he will not place the same value on objects or the senses as he had theretofore. He may in some respects value the sense and object more than before, but the highest value will be given to the subjects and things which he will perceive by his thought.

He hears music or noises or words and tries to appreciate them for their meaning rather than for the manner in which they affect his hearing. If he understands what the meaning and cause of these are, he will value his hearing as an imperfect or true interpreter or sounding board or mirror, and the music or noises or words as the imperfect or true interpretation or echo or reflection. He will value the things or persons from whom these issue none the less because of his understanding the relationships between them. If he can perceive truly in the mental world what a word is and means, he will no longer cling to words and names as he had, though he will now value them more.

His taste is keen for foods, the savor, the bitterness, sweetness, saltness, sourness, the combination of these in foods, but by his taste he tries to perceive to what these reflections refer in the world of thought. If he apprehends what any or all these are in their origin, he will perceive how they, any or all, enter into and give quality to the body of the senses, the linga sharira. He will value his taste the more, the more it is a true recorder of what it reflects.

In smelling he tries to be not affected by the object which he smells, but to perceive in thought, the meaning and character of its odor and its origin. If he can perceive in the world of thought the subject of what he smells, he will apprehend the meaning of the attraction of opposites and their relation in physical forms. Then the objective odors will have less power over him, though his sense of smell may be keener.

The sense of feeling records and senses objects by temperature and by touch. As the aspirant thinks on the subjects of temperature and touch, on pain and pleasure and the causes of these, then instead of trying to be hot or cold or trying to avoid pain or seek pleasure, he learns in the mental world what these subjects mean in themselves and understands the objects of these in the world of the senses to be reflections only. Feeling is then more sensitive, but the objects of feeling have less power over him as he comprehends what they are in the world of thought.

The true aspirant does not try to deny or run away from or suppress the senses; he endeavors to make them true interpreters and reflectors of thoughts. By so doing he learns to separate his thoughts from the senses. Thereby his thoughts gain more freedom of action in the mental world and act independently of the senses. His meditations do not then begin with nor center upon the senses nor the objects of sense for themselves. He tries to begin his meditation with thoughts in themselves (abstract thoughts), not with the senses. As his thoughts become clearer in his own mind he is better able to follow the processes of thought in other minds.

There may be a tendency to argue but should he feel pleasure in getting the best of an argument or in considering another with whom he argues as an opponent, he will make no progress toward discipleship. In speech or argument the self-appointed disciple to the school of the masters must endeavor to speak clearly and truly and to get at and understand the true object of the argument. His object must not be to overcome the other side. He must be as willing to admit his own mistakes and the correctness of another's statements as to stand his own ground when right. By so doing he becomes strong and fearless. If one tries to hold his own in argument he loses sight of or does not see the true and the right, for his purpose in argument is not to uphold the true and right. As he argues to win, he blinds himself to what is true. As he becomes in argument blind to the right, he is more desirous of winning than of seeing the right and he becomes fearful of losing. He who seeks only that which is true and right has no fear, because he cannot lose. He seeks the right and loses nothing if he finds another right.

As the aspirant is able to direct his thoughts forcefully, the power of thought becomes apparent to him. This is a dangerous stage on the road to discipleship. As he thinks clearly he sees that people, circumstances, conditions and environments, may be changed by the nature of his thought. According to the nature of others, he sees that his thought alone, without words, will cause them to respond to or antagonize him. His thought may affect them harmfully. By thought he may affect their bodily ills, by directing them to think about or away from these ills. He finds that he may have added power over the minds of others, by using hypnotism or without its practice. He finds that by his thought he can change his circumstances, that he may increase his income and provide necessaries or luxuries. Change of place and environment will also come in unexpected ways and by unlooked for means. The aspirant who by his thought causes others to act according to his thought, who cures bodily ills, causes bodily harm, or by his thought directs the thought and actions of others, thereby ends his progress on the road to discipleship, and by continuing his endeavor to cure, to heal, to direct and control the thoughts of others, he may attach himself to one of the many sets of beings inimical to humanity—not treated of in this article on adepts, masters and mahatmas.

The aspirant who obtains money by thought, and otherwise than by the means recognized as legitimate business methods, will not become a disciple. He who longs for a change of circumstances and thinks of it only, without doing his best in work to obtain desired circumstances, he who attempts to change his conditions and environments by wishing for and desiring these changes, is made aware that he cannot bring these changes about naturally and that if they are made they will interfere with his progress. He will have experiences to show him that when he fixedly longs and wishes for a change of circumstances or place, the change will come, but with it he will have other and unlooked for things to contend against, which will be as undesirable as those he sought to avoid before. If he does not stop longing for such changes in his circumstances and does not discontinue setting his thought to obtain them, he will never become a disciple. He may appear to obtain what he seeks; his condition and circumstances may be apparently greatly improved, but he will inevitably meet with failure, and that usually in his present life. His thoughts will become confused; his desires turbulent and uncontrolled; he may become a nervous wreck or end in infamy or insanity.

When the self appointed disciple finds that there is an increase in his power of thought and that he may do things by thought, that is a sign that he should not do them. The use of his thought to obtain physical or psychic advantages, debars him from entrance to the school of the masters. He must overcome his thoughts before he can use them. He who thinks he has overcome his thoughts and may use them without harm, is self-deceived and is not fit to enter the mysteries of the world of thought. When the self-appointed disciple finds that he may command others and control conditions by means of thought and does not, then he is on the true path to discipleship. The power of his thought increases.

Endurance, courage, perseverance, determination, perception and enthusiasm are necessary to the aspirant if he wants to become a disciple, but more important than these is the will to be right. Rather had he be right, than in haste. There should be no hurry to be a master; though one should let pass no opportunity for advancement, he should try to live in eternity rather than in the time world. He should search out his motives in thought. He should have his motives right at any cost. It is better to be right at the beginning than wrong at the end of the journey. With an earnest desire for progress, with a constant endeavor to control his thoughts, with a vigilant scrutiny of his motives, and by an impartial judgment and correction of his thoughts and motives when wrong, the aspirant nears discipleship.

At some unexpected moment during his meditations there is a quickening of his thoughts; the circulations of his body cease; his senses are stilled; they offer no resistance or attraction to the mind which acts through them. There is a quickening and gathering of all his thoughts; all thoughts blend into one thought. Thought ceases, but he is conscious. A moment seems to expand to an eternity. He stands within. He has entered consciously into the school of the masters, the mind, and is a truly accepted disciple. He is conscious of one thought and in that all thoughts seem to end. From this one thought he looks through all other thoughts. A flood of light streams through all things and shows them as they are. This may last for hours or days or it may pass within the minute, but during the period the new disciple has found his place of discipleship in the school of the masters.

The circulations of the body start again, the faculties and senses are alive, but there is no disagreement between them. Light streams through them as through all other things. Radiance prevails. Hatred and disagreement have no place, all is a symphony. His experiences in the world continue, but he begins a new life. This life he lives inside his outer life.

His next life is his discipleship. Whatever he was to himself before, he now knows himself to be as a child; but he has no fear. He lives with the confidence of a child in its readiness to learn. He does not use psychic faculties. He has his own life to live. There are many duties for him to perform. No master appears to guide his steps. By his own light he must see his way. He must use his faculties to solve the duties of life as do other men. Though he may not be led into entanglements, he is not free from them. He has no powers or cannot use them otherwise than as an ordinary man to avoid obstacles or adverse conditions of physical life. He does not meet at once other disciples of the school of the masters; nor does he receive instruction as to what he shall do. He is alone in the world. No friends or relations will understand him; the world cannot understand him. He may be considered as wise or simple, as rich or poor, as natural or strange, by those he meets. Each one sees him to be what that one himself seeks to be, or as the opposite.

The disciple in the school of the masters is given no rules to live by. He has but one rule, one set of instructions; this is that by which he found entrance to discipleship. This rule is the one thought into which all other thoughts entered; it is that thought through which his other thoughts are clearly seen. This one thought is that by which he learns the way. He may not at all times act from this thought. It may be seldom that he can act from this thought; but he cannot forget it. When he can see it, no difficulty is too great to overcome, no trouble is too hard to bear, no misery can cause despair, no sorrow is too heavy to carry, no joy will overwhelm, no position too high or low to fill, no responsibility too onerous to assume. He knows the way. By this thought he stills all other thoughts. By this thought the light comes, the light which floods the world and shows all things as they are.

Although the new disciple knows of no other disciples, although no masters come to him, and although he seems to be alone in the world, he is not really alone. He may be unnoticed by men, but he is not unnoticed by the masters.

The disciple should not expect direct instruction from a master within a given time; it will not come until he is ready to receive it. He knows that he does not know when that time shall be, but he knows that it will be. The disciple may continue to the end of the life in which he becomes disciple without consciously meeting with other disciples; but before he passes from the present life he will know his master.

During his life as disciple he can expect no such early experiences as those of the disciple in the school of the adepts. When he is fitted he enters into personal relationship with others in his set of disciples and meets his master, whom he knows. There is no strangeness in the meeting of his master. It is as natural as the knowing of mother and of father. The disciple feels an intimate reverence for his teacher, but does not stand in worshipful awe of him.

The disciple learns that through all grades, the school of the masters is in the school of the world. He sees that the masters and disciples watch over mankind, though, like a child, mankind is not aware of this. The new disciple sees that masters do not attempt to curb mankind, nor to change the conditions of men.

The disciple is given as his work to live unknown in the lives of men. He may be sent into the world again to live with men, to aid them in the enactment of just laws whenever the desires of men will permit of it. In doing this he is shown by his teacher the karma of his land or the land to which he goes, and is a conscious assistant in the adjustment of the karma of a nation. He sees that a nation is a larger individual, that as the nation rules its subjects, so it will be ruled itself by its subjects, that if it lives by war it will also die by war, that as it treats those whom it conquers, so will it be treated when it is conquered, that its period of existence as a nation will be in proportion to its industry and care of its subjects, especially its weak, its poor, its helpless, and that its life will be prolonged if it has ruled in peace and justice.

As to his family and friends, the disciple sees the relationship which he bore towards them in former lives; he sees his duties, the result of these. All this he sees, but not with psychic eyes. Thought is the means he works with and thoughts he sees as things. As the disciple progresses, he may by thinking on any object trace it back to its source.

By meditation on his body and its different parts, he learns the different uses to which each organ may be put. By dwelling on each organ he sees in them the action of other worlds. By dwelling on the fluids of the body he learns of the circulation and distribution of the waters of the earth. By brooding on the airs of the body he perceives the currents in the ether of space. By meditating on the breath he may perceive the forces, or principles, their origin, and their action. By meditating on the body as a whole he may observe time, in its arrangements, grouping, relations, changes and transformations, in three of the manifested worlds. By meditating on the physical body as a whole he may observe the arrangement of the physical universe. By meditating on the psychic form body he will perceive the dream world, with its reflections and desires. By meditating on his thought body, he apprehends the heaven world and the ideals of the world of men. By meditation on and understanding of his bodies, the disciple learns how he should treat each of these bodies. What he had before heard concerning the chastity of the physical body—in order that he may come to self knowledge,—that he now clearly perceives. Having comprehended by observation and meditation the changes which go on in the physical body by the processes of digestion and assimilation of foods and having observed the relationship between the physical, psychic and mental and the alchemization of foods into essences, and having seen the plan of the work with its processes, he begins his work.

While strictly observing the laws of his land, fulfilling the duties of position to family and friends, he begins intelligently to work with and in his body, though he may have tried before. In his meditations and observations, thought and the faculties of his mind have been used, not faculties of the psychic senses. The disciple attempts no control of elemental fires, directs no currents of the winds, attempts no searches of the waters, makes no excursions into the earth, for all these he sees in his bodies. He watches their courses and nature by his thought. He attempts no interference with these powers outside himself, but directs and controls their action in his bodies according to the universal plan. As he controls their action in his body he knows that he may control those forces in themselves, but he makes no such attempt. No rules are given him, for the rules are seen in the actions of the forces. The races preceding his physical race are seen and their history is known, as he becomes acquainted with his physical body, his psychic form body, his life body and his breath body. The physical, the form and life bodies he may know. The breath body he cannot yet know. It is beyond him. Minerals, plants and animals are found within his form. The essences which are compounded from these may be observed in the secretions of his body.

One thing he has within him which it is his work to control. This is the unformed elemental desire, which is a cosmic principle and which it is his duty to overcome. He sees that it is as unconquerable to the one who tries to starve and kill it, as it is to him who feeds and satiates it. The lower must be overcome by the higher; the disciple subdues his desire as he controls his thoughts. He sees that desire can have no thing without the thought to procure it. If the thought is of the desire, the desire will guide the thought; but if the thought is of thought or of the real, the desire must reflect it. Desire is seen to be fashioned by thought when thought dwells calmly in itself. Restless and turbulent at first, the desires are quelled and subdued as the disciple continues to exercise his thought and to bring the faculties of his mind to their fruition. He continues to think of himself in the mental world; thus he controls desire by his thoughts.

If he remains in the world fulfilling his duties to and among men, he may fill a prominent or obscure position, but he allows no wastes in his life. He does not indulge in oratory nor long dissertations, unless advised to do so. Speech is controlled, as are other habits of life and thought, but in controlling habits he must be as inconspicuous as his position will allow. When he is able to live without longing for and without regrets at leaving the world, when he appreciates that time is in eternity, and that eternity is through time, and that he may live in eternity while in time, and if his turn of life has not been passed, he is aware that the period of outer action is ended and the period of inner action begins.

His work is finished. The scene shifts. His part in that act of the drama of life is over. He retires behind the scenes. He passes into retirement and goes through a process analogous to that through which the disciple for adeptship passed in becoming an adept. The bodies or races which in ordinary men are blended with the physical have during his preparation in the world become distinct. The physical counterparts are strong and healthy. His nervous organization has been well strung on the sounding board of his body and responds to the lightest and most vigorous play of the thoughts which sweep over it. Harmonies of thought play over the nerves of his body and stimulate and direct the essences of the body through channels which until now had not been opened. The circulations of the seminal principle are turned into these channels; new life is given to the body. A body which seemed aged, may be restored to the freshness and vigor of manhood. The vital essences are no longer drawn by desire to act in the outer physical world, they are led by thought in preparation for entrance into the higher world of thought.

(To be continued)

ADEPTS, MASTERS AND MAHATMAS

(Continued)

[From *The Word,* Vol. 10 No. 6, March 1910]

THE physical body is the ground in which the new body from the seed of the mind begins to grow. The head of the physical is the heart of the new body and it lives throughout the physical body. It is not physical; it is not psychic; it is pure life and pure thought. During the early period which follows the growth and development of this body, the disciple will meet with masters and with adepts and see the places they frequent and the people whom they rule; but that with which the disciple's thought is most concerned, is the new world which is opening to him.

In the school of the masters the disciple now learns of the states after death and before birth. He understands how after death the mind, which was incarnate, leaves the flesh of earth, throws off gradually the lurid cloaks of its desires and awakens to its heaven world; how, as the coils of fleshly desires fall away the excarnate mind becomes forgetful and unaware of them. The disciple understands the heaven world of the human mind; that the thoughts which were not of a fleshly or sensual nature which were held during life, are those of man's heaven world and make up man's heaven world; that those beings and persons who were connected with his ideals while the man was in the physical body, are with him in ideal in his heaven world; but only in so far as they were of the ideal and not of the flesh. He understands that the length of the period of the heaven world depends upon and is determined by the scope of the ideals and the amount of strength and thought which were given to the ideals by man while in the physical body; that with high ideals and strong desires for their attainment the heaven world lasts longer, while the lighter or shallower the ideal and the less strength given to it, the shorter is the heaven world. It is perceived that time of the heaven world is different from time in the astral desire world or time of the physical world. Time of the heaven world is of the nature of its thoughts. Time of the astral world is measured by the changes of desire. Whereas, time in the physical world is reckoned by the movement of the earth among the stars and the occurrence of events. He understands that the heaven of the excarnate mind does come to an end and must come to an end because the ideals are exhausted and because no new ideals can be there formulated, but only such are there as were held while man was in a physical body. The disciple comprehends how the mind leaves its plane; how it attracts the old tendencies and desires of physical life which had been resolved into something akin to seeds; how these old tendencies are drawn into the new form designed during its past life; how the form becomes associated with and enters through the breath the forms of the parents to be; how the form as a seed enters the matrix of the mother and how this formative seed passes across or grows up through the different kingdoms during the process of its gestation; how after assuming its human shape it is born into the world and how the mind incarnates into that form through the breath. All this the disciple sees, but not with his physical eyes nor with any clairvoyant sense of sight. This the disciple in the school of the masters sees by means of his mind and not by his senses. This the disciple understands because it is seen by and with the mind and not through the senses. To see this clairvoyantly would be as seeing it through a colored glass. All that is perceived and understood by the disciple is perceived while he is in his physical body and in possession of his normal faculties and senses.

The disciple now understands that what he thus perceives has been to some degree passed through by himself before his retirement from the busy world of men and he clearly understands that what the ordinary man experiences or passes through only after death, he must in future pass through while fully conscious in his physical body. In order to become a disciple he has passed through and experienced the astral desire world before leaving the world. He must now learn to live consciously in and operate from the heaven world of man in order to become a master. Experiencing the astral desire world does not mean that he lives consciously in the astral world, using clairvoyant or other psychic senses, in the same way as an adept or his disciple, but it means that he experiences the astral world with all of its forces, through certain temptations, attractions, pleasures, fears, hatreds, sorrows, which all disciples in the school of the masters must experience and overcome before they can be accepted and know of their acceptance as disciples in the school of the masters.

While still a disciple, the heaven world of man is not clear and distinct to him; this can only be realized fully by a master. But the disciple is informed by his master concerning the heaven world and the faculties which he must bring into use and perfect in order that he may be more than a learner in the heaven world.

The heaven world of man is the mental world into which the disciple is learning to enter consciously and in which a master lives consciously at all times. To live consciously in the mental world, the mind must build for itself a body of and suited to the mental world. This the disciple knows that he must do, and that only by the doing of it will he enter the mental world. As disciple he must have desire largely under his control. But as disciple only he has not mastered it nor learned how to direct it intelligently as a force distinct from himself and his thoughts. The coils of desire are still about him and prevent the full development and use of his mental faculties. As the mind separates from its desires after death in order to enter its heaven world, so now the disciple must grow out of desire by which he is surrounded or in which he, as a thinking entity, is immersed.

He now learns that at the time of becoming a disciple and during the moment or period of that calm ecstasy, there entered into the inner chambers of his brain a seed or germ of light which was really the cause of the quickening of his thoughts and the stilling of his body, and that at that time he had conceived of a new life and that from that conception is to be developed and born intelligently into the mental world the body which will make of him a master, the master body.

Like the disciple in the school of the adepts, he, too, passes through a period analogous to that of man and woman during foetal development. But though the process is similar the results are different. The woman is unconscious of the process and the laws connected with it. The disciple of the adepts is aware of the process; he must obey certain rules during his period of gestation and he is assisted in his birth by an adept.

The disciple of the masters is aware of the periods and processes but he has no rules given him. His thoughts are his rules.

He must learn these himself. He judges these thoughts and their effects by calling into use the one thought which judges other thoughts impartially. He is aware of the gradual development of the body which will make him more than man and he is aware that he must be conscious of the stages of its development. Though woman and the disciple of the adepts may and do by their attitude assist in the development of the bodies to which they will give birth, yet these continue to develop by natural causes and influences and will be completely formed without their direct supervision. Not so with the disciple of the masters. He must himself bring the new body to its birth. This new body is not a physical body as is that born of the woman and which has physical organs, nor is it like the desire body of the adept which has no organs such as those used in the physical body for digestion, but which has the form of the physical though it is not physical, and has organs of sense such as the eye, or ear, though these, of course, are not physical.

The body of the master to be will not be physical, nor will it have a physical form. The master body has faculties, rather than senses and organs. The disciple becomes conscious of the body developing through him as he tries and is able to develop and to use his mental faculties. His body develops as he continues and learns to use his faculties intelligently. These faculties are not the senses nor are they connected with the senses, though they are analogous to the senses and are used in the mental world similarly as the senses are used in the astral world, and the organs in the physical world. The ordinary man uses his senses and faculties, but is ignorant as to what the senses are in themselves and what his mental faculties are and is quite unaware of how he thinks, what his thoughts are, how they are developed, and how his mental faculties act in connection with or through his senses and organs. The ordinary man makes no distinction between his many mental faculties. The disciple of the masters must be not only aware of the difference and distinctions between his mental faculties, but he must act with these as clearly and intelligently in the mental world as the ordinary man now acts through his sense organs in the physical world.

For each sense every man has a corresponding mental faculty, but only a disciple will know how to distinguish between the faculty and the sense and how to use his mental faculties independently of the senses. By trying to use his mental faculties independently of his senses, the disciple becomes disentangled from the world of desire in which he still is and from which he must pass. As he continues his efforts he learns the mental articulation of his faculties and sees definitely what these are. The disciple is shown that all things which are in the physical world and the astral desire world receive their ideal types in the mental world as emanations from the eternal ideas in the spiritual world. He understands that every subject in the mental world is only a connection of matter according to an idea in the spiritual world. He perceives that the senses by which a physical object or an astral object is seen are the astral mirror on which are reflected, through its physical organ, the physical objects which are seen, and that the object which is seen is appreciated only when the sense is receptive to and can also reflect the type in the mental world, of which the object in the physical world is a copy. This reflection from the mental world is had by means of a certain mental faculty which relates the object in the physical world with its type as subject in the mental world.

The disciple sees the objects and senses the things in the physical world, but he interprets them by using his respective mental faculties and by turning the faculties to the respective types of the objects of the physical world, instead of attempting to understand the objects of the senses by means of the senses. As his experiences continue he appreciates the being of mind as independent of the five senses and of sense perceptions. He knows that true knowledge of the senses can be had only by the faculties of the mind, and that the objects of the senses or the senses can never be known truly while the faculties of the mind function through the senses and their physical organs. He perceives truly that the knowledge of all things of the physical world and of the astral desire world is learned only in the mental world, and that this learning must take place in the mental world by calling into use the faculties of the mind independently of the physical body, and that these faculties of the mind are used consciously and with greater accuracy and precision than it is possible to use the physical sense organs and astral senses.

Confusion prevails in the many schools of philosophical speculation, which have attempted to explain the mind and its operations by sensuous perceptions. The disciple sees that it is impossible for a thinker to perceive the order of universal phenomena with their causes, because, although the speculator is often able to rise to the mental world through one of his mental faculties and there to apprehend one of the truths of existence, he is unable to maintain the unclouded use of the faculty until he is fully conscious of what he apprehends, though his apprehensions are so strong that he will always be of the opinion which is formed from such apprehensions. Further, that when this faculty is again active in his senses he tries to square what he has apprehended in the mental world by his mental faculties as they now act through their respective senses. The result is that what he may have truly apprehended in the mental world is contradicted or confused by the coloring, atmosphere, intervention and evidences of his senses.

The world has been and is to-day undecided as to what the mind is. Various opinions prevail as to whether the mind is prior to or the result of physical organization and action. Although there is no general agreement as to whether mind has separate entity and body, there is a definition which is usually accepted as a definition of the mind. This is its usual form: "Mind is the sum of the states of consciousness made up of thought, will, and feeling." This definition seems to have settled the question for many thinkers, and to have relieved them of the need to define. Some have become so enchanted with the definition that they summon it to their defence or wield it as a magic formula to clear away the difficulties of any psychological subject which may arise. The definition is pleasing as a formula and familiar because of its customary sound, but insufficient as a definition. "Mind is the sum of the states of consciousness made up of thought, will and feeling," charms the ear, but when the light of the enquiring mind is turned on it, the charm has gone, and in its place there is an empty form. The three factors are thought, will and feeling, and the mind is said to experience states of consciousness. What these factors are is not settled among those who accept the formula, and although the phrase "states of consciousness" is so frequently used, consciousness is not known in itself, and the states into which it is claimed that Consciousness is divided or apportioned have no reality as Consciousness. They are not Consciousness. Consciousness has no states. Consciousness is One. It is not to be divided or numbered by degree or classed by state or condition. Like lenses of different colors through which the one light is seen, so the faculties of the mind or the senses, according to their coloring and degree of development, apprehend Consciousness to be of the color or quality or development through which it is apprehended; whereas, irrespective of the coloring senses or qualities of mind, and though present through and in all things, Consciousness remains One, unchanged and without attributes. Although philosophers think, they do not know what thought is essentially nor the processes of thought, unless they can use the mental faculties independent of the senses. So that thought is not generally known nor its nature agreed upon by the philosophers of the schools. Will is a subject which has concerned philosophical minds. Will in its own state is farther removed and more obscure than thought, because will in its own state cannot be known until the mind has first developed all its faculties and become free from them. Feeling is one of the senses, and is not a faculty of the mind. The mind has a faculty which is related to and in the ordinary man operates through his sense of feeling, but feeling is not a faculty of the mind. It cannot be truly said that "Mind is the sum of the states of consciousness made up of thought, will and feeling."

The disciple in the school of the masters does not concern himself with any of the speculations of the schools of philosophy. He may see by their teachings that the founders of some of the schools which are still known to the world, used their mental faculties independently of their senses, and used them freely in the mental world and could coordinate and use them through their senses. The disciple must come into knowledge through his own mental faculties and these he acquires gradually and by his own effort.

Every natural human now has seven senses, though he is supposed to have only five. These are the sight, hearing, taste, smell, touch, moral and "I" senses. The first four of these have as their respective organs of sense, the eye, ear, tongue and nose, and represent the order of involution into body. Touch or feeling is the fifth and is common to the senses. These five belong to the animal nature of man. The moral sense is the sixth sense and is used only by the mind; it is not of the animal. The "I" sense, or sense of Ego, is the mind sensing itself. These last three, touch, moral and I senses, represent the evolution and the developing of the mind of the animal. The animal is prompted to the use of its five senses, as sight, hearing, tasting, smelling and touching, by natural impulse and without regard to any moral sense, which it has not, unless it is a domestic animal and under the influence of the human mind, which to some degree it may reflect. The I sense becomes manifest through the moral sense. The I sense is the sensing of the mind in and by the body. The touch, moral and I senses act in connection with the other four and with the body as a whole rather than with any part or organ of the body. Although there are organs through which they may act, yet so far no organs have become specialized, which can be used intelligently by their respective senses.

Corresponding to the senses are the faculties of the mind. The faculties of the mind may be called the light, time, image, focus, dark, motive and I-am faculties. Every human has these faculties and uses them in a more or less indistinct and immature way.

No man can have any mental perception without his light faculty. Movement and order, change and rhythm cannot be understood nor used without the time faculty. Figure and color and matter can not be conceived, related and pictured without the image faculty. No body or picture or color or movement or problem can be approximated or grasped without the focus faculty. Contact, union, concealment, obscuration and transformation cannot be effected without the dark faculty. Progress, development, ambition, competition, aspiration, would be impossible without the motive faculty. Identity, continuity, permanence would have no meaning, and knowledge could not be acquired without the I-am faculty. Without the I-am faculty there would be no power of reflection, no purpose in life, no strength nor beauty nor proportion in forms, no grasp of conditions and environments nor the power to change them, for man would be an animal only.

Man uses these faculties though he is not aware of how or to what degree he uses them. In some men one or several of the faculties are more developed than the others, which remain dormant. Seldom is there a man who has or tries to have an even development of his faculties. Those who devote their energies to specialize in one or two of the faculties without regard to the others will, in the course of time, be geniuses of the faculties specialized, though their other faculties may be stunted and dwarfed. The man who has due regard for all the faculties of his mind may seem backward in development as compared with those who excel in specialties, but while he continues his development evenly and steadily these special geniuses will be found to be mentally unbalanced and unfit to meet the requirements on the path of attainment.

The disciple in the school of the masters understands that he should develop his faculties evenly and orderly, though he, too, has the choice of specializing in some and disregarding others. So he may disregard the image and dark faculties and develop the others; in that case he would disappear from the world of men. Or he might disregard all faculties except the light and I-am and focus faculties; in that case he would develop an overmastering egotism and blend the focus faculty in the light and I-am faculties and disappear from the world of men and the ideal mental world, and remain throughout the evolution in the spiritual world. He may develop one or more of the faculties, singly or in combination, and act in the world or worlds corresponding to the faculty or faculties of his choice. It is made plain to the disciple that his particular faculty through which he will become from a disciple in the school of the masters, a master, is the motive faculty. By the motive faculty he will declare himself. Of all things motives are the most important.

During his experience and through his duties in the world the disciple has learned much of the course of development through which he must pass. But as disciple retired from the world and living alone or in a community in which there are other disciples, he begins to do that which he had apprehended or about which he had been informed while in the world. The reality of himself is more evident to him. He is aware of the reality of his faculties, but he has not yet realized the full and free use of these and the identity of himself. That which entered into him on becoming a disciple, that is, the seed and the process of its development, is becoming evident to him. As it becomes evident the faculties are used more freely. If the disciple chooses a development in conformity with universal law and without the motive for development for himself alone, then all the faculties unfold and develop naturally and orderly.

While in his physical body, the disciple learns gradually of the potential power of the I-am faculty within. This is learned by calling into use the light faculty. The power of the I-am faculty is learned through the power of the light faculty. But it is learned only as the disciple develops and is able to use his focus faculty. With the continued use of the focus faculty, the I-am and the light powers vivify the motive and the time faculties. The exercise of the motive faculty develops quality and purpose in the I-am faculty. The time faculty gives movement and growth. The focus faculty adjusts the powers of the motive and time faculties to the I-am faculty in its light power, which becomes more evident. The dark faculty tends to disrupt, envelop, confuse and obscure the light faculty as it, the dark faculty, is awakened or called into use. But as the focus faculty is exercised, the dark faculty acts with the image faculty, and the image faculty causes to come into a body the I-am in its light power. By the use of the focus faculty the other faculties are adjusted into a body. With his faculties awakened and acting harmoniously, the disciple, in proportion as that which is developing within comes into being, learns respecting the knowledge of the worlds in which or through which they operate.

The light faculty makes known a limitless sphere of light. What this light is, is not at once known. By the use of the light faculty all things are resolved into light. By the use of the light faculty all things are made known to or through the other faculties.

The time faculty reports matter in its revolutions, combinations, separations and changes. Through the time faculty is made clear the nature of matter; the measure of all bodies and the dimension or dimensions of each, the measure of their existence and their relationship to each other. The time faculty measures the ultimate divisions of matter, or the ultimate divisions of time. Through the time faculty is made plain that the ultimate divisions of matter are the ultimate divisions of time.

Through the image faculty, matter takes form. The image faculty intercepts particles of matter which it coordinates, shapes and holds. By the use of the image faculty unformed nature is brought into form and species are preserved.

The focus faculty gathers, adjusts, relates and centralizes things. By means of the focus faculty duality becomes unity.

The dark faculty is a sleeping power. When aroused, the dark faculty is restless and energetic and opposed to order. The dark faculty is a sleep producing power. The dark faculty is aroused by the use of other faculties which it negatives and resists. The dark faculty blindly interferes with and obscures all other faculties and things.

The motive faculty chooses, decides and directs by its decision. Through the motive faculty, silent orders are given which are the causes of the coming into existence of all things. The motive faculty gives direction to the particles of matter which are compelled to come into form according to the direction given them. The use of the motive faculty is the cause of every result in any world, however remote. The use of the motive faculty puts into operation all the causes which bring about and determine all results in the phenomenal and any other worlds. By use of the motive faculty the degree and attainment of all beings of intelligence is determined. Motive is the creative cause of every action.

The I-am faculty is that by which all things are known, it is the knowing faculty. The I-am faculty is that by which the identity of the I-am is known and by which its identity is made distinct from other intelligences. By means of the I-am faculty identity is given to matter. The I-am faculty is the faculty of being conscious of self.

The disciple becomes aware of these faculties and the uses to which they may be put. Then he begins the exercise and training of them. The course of exercising and training these faculties is carried on while the disciple is in the physical body, and by that training and development he regulates, adapts and adjusts the faculties into the body which is coming into being through him, and on the development and birth of which he will become a master. The disciple is conscious of the light faculty, of the I-am faculty, of the time faculty, of the motive faculty, of the image faculty, of the dark faculty, but as disciple he must begin his work by and through the focus faculty.

(To be continued)

ADEPTS, MASTERS AND MAHATMAS

(Continued)

[From *The Word,* Vol. 11 No. 1, April 1910]

WHAT the disciple had before learned while in contact with the men of the world he now verifies to be true or false by bringing the faculties of his mind to bear on whatever subject is considered. The disciple finds that that thought into which all other thoughts had blended and by which he had found himself as disciple, and had known himself to be an accepted disciple in the school of the masters, was in fact the opening up of and ability to use his focus faculty consciously; that he had, after his long and continued efforts, been able to bring together his wandering thoughts which had been attracted by and were operating through his senses, was due to the use of his focus faculty; that by the focus faculty he had collected and centered those thoughts and so quieted the activities of the mind as to allow the light faculty to inform him where he was and of his entrance into the mental world. He sees that he could not then use his focus faculty and light faculty continuously, and that to be a master he must be able to use the five lower faculties, the time, image, focus, dark and motive faculties consciously, intelligently and at will as continuously as he may decide.

When the disciple begins to use his focus faculty intelligently it seems to him as though he is coming into great knowledge and that he will enter all realms in the different worlds by the use of his focus faculty. It seems to him that he is able to know everything and answer any question by using his focus faculty, and all the faculties seem to be at his disposal and ready for his use, when operated from his focus faculty, so that when he would know by any subject the meaning or nature of any object or thing, he centralizes the aforenamed faculties on that subject, which he holds steadily in mind by his focus faculty. As by the focus faculty he holds the subject and draws the other faculties to bear on it, the I-am faculty brings the light, the motive faculty directs matter by the time faculty into the image faculty, and all these together overcome the dark faculty, and out of the darkness which had obscured the mind the object or thing appears and is known in its subjective state, in all that it is or may be. This is done by the disciple at any time and anywhere while in his physical body.

The disciple is able to go through this process in the course of one inhalation and exhalation of his natural breathing without stoppage. As he gazes at any thing or hears any sound or tastes of any food or senses any odor or contacts any thing or thinks of any thought, he is able to find out the meaning and nature of that which has been suggested to him through his senses or by the faculties of the mind, according to the nature and kind of motive which directs the inquiry. The focus faculty acts in the physical body from the region of sex, libra (♎). Its corresponding sense is the sense of smell. The body and all the elements of the body are changed during one inbreathing and outbreathing. One inbreathing and outbreathing are only half of one complete round of the circle of breath. This half of the circle of breath is taken in through the nose and lungs and heart and goes in the blood to the organs of sex. This is the physical half of the breath. The other half of the breath enters the blood through the organ of sex and returns by the blood to the heart through the lungs and is exhaled through the tongue or the nose. Between these swings of the physical and magnetic breath there is a moment of balance; at this moment of balance all objects or things become known to the disciple by the use of his focus faculty.

The experience which made of the disciple a disciple put him in possession and gave him the use of the focus faculty, and with that first use of this faculty the disciple began its conscious and intelligent use. Before its first use the disciple was like an infant which, though having the organs of sense, is not yet possessed of its senses. When an infant is born, and for some time after its birth, it cannot see objects though its eyes are open. It senses a buzzing sound though it knows not whence comes the sound. It takes its mother's milk, but has no sense of taste. Odors enter through the nose, but it cannot smell. It touches and feels, but cannot localize the feeling; and altogether the infant is an uncertain and unhappy waif of the senses. Objects are held before it to attract its notice, and at some time the little thing is able to bring its eyes to a focus on some object. There is a moment of joy when the object is seen. The little thing sees into the world of its birth. It is no longer a waif in the world, but a citizen of it. It becomes a member of society when it knows its mother and is able to relate its organs to the objects of sense. That by which it was able to bring the organs of sight, hearing and of the other senses in line with the object seen, heard or otherwise sensed, was the power of focus. Every human who comes into the physical world must go through the processes of relating his organs of sense and his senses to the things of sense. Nearly all men forget the first object seen, forget the first sound heard, do not remember the things first tasted, what odor it was that was first smelled, how they got into touch with the world; and most men have forgotten how the focus faculty was used and how they still use the focus faculty by which they sense the world and the things of the world. But the disciple does not forget the one thought into which all his thoughts had been centered and by which he seemed to know all things and by which he knew himself as an accepted disciple.

He knows that it was by the focus faculty that he knew himself to be in another world than the world of the senses, though he was in the senses, even as the infant discovered itself in the physical world when it was able to focus its organs of sense in the world of the senses. And so having intelligent use of this faculty the disciple is as a child in relation to the mental world, which he is learning to enter through his faculties, by means of his focus faculty. All his faculties are adjusted to each other by means of his focus faculty. This focus faculty is the power of the mind to bring in line and relate any thing to its origin and source. By holding a thing in the mind and by use of the focus faculty, on and in that thing, it is made known as it is, and the process through which it became as it is, and also what it may become. When a thing is directly in line with its origin and source it is known as it is. By the focus faculty he can trace the path and events by which a thing has become as it is through the past, and by that faculty he can also trace the path of that thing to the time when it will have to decide for itself what it chooses to be. The focus faculty is the range finder between objects and subjects and between subjects and ideas; that is to say, the focus faculty brings into line any object of the senses in the physical world with its subject in the mental world and brings into line through the subject in the mental world the idea in the spiritual world, which is the origin and source of the object or thing and of all its kind. The focus faculty is like a sun-glass which gathers rays of light and centers them at a point, or like a searchlight which shows the way through the surrounding fog or darkness. The focus faculty is of a vortex-like power which centers movements into sound, or causes sound to be known by shapes or figures. The focus faculty is like an electric spark which centers two elements into water or by which water is changed into gases. The focus faculty is like an invisible magnet which attracts and draws in and holds in itself to itself fine particles which it shows in a body or form.

The disciple uses the focus faculty as one would use a field glass to bring objects into view. When one places a field glass to his eyes, nothing is at first seen, but as he regulates the lenses between the objects and his eyes the field of vision becomes less foggy. Gradually the objects take on outline and when they are focussed they are plainly seen. In like manner, the disciple turns his focus faculty on the thing which he would know and that thing becomes more and more clear until the moment of focus, when the thing is adjusted to its subject and is made plain and clear to and is understood by the mind. The balance wheel by which an object is made known to the mind by means of the focus faculty is the wheel or circle of the breath. The focus faculty is in focus at the moment of balance between the normal inbreath and outbreath.

The disciple is happy in this period of his life. He is asking and knows of objects and things in the physical world and their causes in the mental world; this affords happiness. He is in the childhood of his discipleship and enjoys all experiences in his retirement from the world, as a child enjoys itself in the life of the world and before the hardships of life have begun. The sky shows him the plan of creation. The wind sings to him its history the song of life in the constantly flowing time. The rains and the waters open to him and inform him how the formless seeds of life are carried into form, how all things are replenished and nourished by water and how by the taste which water gives, all plants select their food and grow. By her perfumes and odors, earth discloses to the disciple how she attracts and repels, how one and one become blended into one, how and by what means and for what purpose all things come or pass through the body of man and how heaven and earth unite to temper and test and balance the mind of man. And so in the child-hood of his discipleship the disciple sees the colors of nature in their true light, hears the music of her voice, drinks in the beauty of her forms and finds himself encircled by her fragrance.

The childhood of discipleship ends. Through his senses he has read the book of nature in the terms of the mind. He has been mentally happy in his companionship with nature. He tries to use his faculties without using his senses, and he tries to know himself as distinct from all his senses. From his body of sex, he trains the range of his focus faculty to find the mental world. This puts him out of range of the senses in the physical body, though he is still possessed of his senses. As he continues to so use his focus faculty, one after another the senses are stilled. The disciple cannot touch or feel, he cannot smell, he has no sense of taste, all sounds have ceased, vision is gone, he cannot see and darkness surrounds him; yet he is conscious. This moment, when the disciple is conscious without seeing or hearing or tasting or smelling and without touching or feeling anything, is of vital importance. What will fol-low this moment of being conscious without the senses? Some keen minds in the world have tried to find this state of being conscious without the senses. Some have shrunk back with horror when they had almost found it. Others have gone mad. Only one who has been long trained in and who has been tempered by the senses can remain steadily conscious during that crucial moment.

What follows the experience of the disciple has already been decided by his motives in attempting it. The disciple comes out of the experience a changed man. The experience may only have been for a second by the time of his senses, but it may have seemed an eternity to that which was conscious in the experience. During that moment the disciple has learned the secret of death, but he has not mastered death. That which was steadily conscious for a moment independently of the senses is to the disciple like coming to life in the mental world. The disciple has stood in the entrance to the heaven world, but he has not entered it. The heaven world of the mind cannot be joined to or made one with the world of the senses, though they are related to each other as opposites. The world of the mind is dreadful to a thing of the senses. The world of the senses is as hell to the purified mind.

When the disciple is able he will again repeat the experiment which he has learned. Whether the experiment is dreaded or is eagerly sought by him, it will lead the disciple into a period of negation and darkness. The physical body of the disciple has become a thing distinct from himself though he is still in it. By the use of his focus faculty in attempting to enter the mental or heaven world he called into action the dark faculty of the mind.

The experience of being conscious without seeing, hearing, tasting, smelling, touching and feeling is a mental demonstration to the disciple of all he has previously thought and heard concerning the reality of the mental world and of its being different and distinct from the physical and astral worlds. This experience is thus far the reality of his life, and is unlike any previous experience. It has shown him how little and transitory is his physical body and it has given him a taste or prescience of immortality. It has given him distinctness of being from his physical body and from sensuous perceptions, and yet he does not really know who or what he is, though he knows he is not the physical or astral form. The disciple realizes that he cannot die, though his physical body is to him a thing of change. The experience of being conscious without the senses gives the disciple great strength and power, but it also ushers him into a period of unutterable gloom. This gloom is caused by the awakening into action of the dark faculty as it had never before acted.

Through all periods and existences of the mind the dark faculty of the mind had been sluggish and slow, like a gorged boa or a serpent in the cold. The dark faculty, blind itself, had caused blindness to the mind; itself deaf, it had caused a confusion of sounds to the senses and dulled the understanding; without form and color, it had prevented or interfered with the mind and senses from perceiving beauty and from giving shape to unformed matter; without balance and having no judgment it has dulled the instincts of the senses and prevented the mind from being one-pointed. It had been unable to touch or feel anything, and had bewildered the mind and produced doubt and uncertainty in the sense. Having neither thought nor judgment it prevented reflection, blunted the mind and obscured the causes of action. Unreasoning and without identity it opposed reason, was an obstacle to knowledge and prevented the mind from knowing its identity.

Although having no senses and opposed to the other faculties of the mind, the presence of the dark faculty had kept the senses in activity, and allowed them or aided them to cloud or obscure the faculties of the mind. It had fed in the senses the activities which have paid it constant tribute, and that tribute had kept it in a torpid state. But the disciple trying to overcome the senses and to enter the mental world has in great degree withheld tribute from this thing of ignorance, the dark faculty of the mind. By his many efforts toward overcoming and control of his desires, the disciple had seemingly stilled the dark faculty and had seemingly enjoyed the use of his other faculties in interpreting his senses. But he finds that his desires were not really conquered and the dark faculty of the mind was not really overcome. When the disciple was able to be conscious without the use and independently of his senses, he called at that time and by that experience the dark faculty of his mind into activity as never before.

This, the dark faculty of his mind, is the adversary of the disciple. The dark faculty has now the strength of the world serpent. It has in it the ignorance of the ages, but also the cunning and wiles and glamour and deception of all bygone times. Before this awakening, the dark faculty was senseless, sluggish and without reason, and it still is. It sees without eyes, hears without ears, and is possessed of senses keener than any known to physical man, and it makes use of all the wiles of thought without thinking. It acts directly and in a way most likely to overcome and prevent the disciple from crossing through its realm of death into the mental world of immortal life.

The disciple has known of the dark faculty and been informed of its wiles and of having to meet and overcome them. But that old evil, the dark faculty, seldom attacks the disciple in the way he expects to be met, if he does expect. It has innumerable wiles and subtle ways of attacking and opposing the disciple. There are only two means which it can employ, and it invariably uses the second only if the first has failed.

After being conscious without the senses, the disciple is more sensitive to the world than ever before. But he is so in a different manner than before. He is aware of the inside of things. Rocks and trees are so many living things not seen, but apprehended as such. All the elements speak to him, and it seems to him that he may command them. The world seems a living, throbbing, being. The earth seems to move with the movement of his body. The trees seem to bend to his nod. The seas seem to moan and the tides to rise and fall with the beating of his heart and the waters to circulate with the circulation of his blood. The winds seem to come and go in rhythmic movement with his breath and all seems to be kept in movement by his energy.

This the disciple experiences by being aware of it rather than sensing it. But at some time while he is aware of all this, his inner senses spring into life and he sees and senses the inner world of which he had been aware mentally. This world seems to open out to him or to grow out of and include and beautify and enliven the old physical world. Colors and tones and figures and forms are more harmoniously beautiful and exquisite and immeasurably more delightful than any the physical world did offer. All this is his and all things seem to be for him alone to direct and use. He seems the king and ruler of nature which had been waiting for him through the ages until he should, as now, at last have come to rule in her kingdoms. All the senses of the disciple in the school of the masters are now keyed to their highest pitch. In the midst of the delights of sense, there comes to the disciple one thought. It is the thought by which he sees through things and knows them as they are. By it, the disciple in the school of the masters knows that the new world in which he stands is not the world of the masters, the mental world, beautiful though it is. As he is about to pass judgment on this glorified world, the world of the inner senses, figures and forms and all elements cry out to him. First to enjoy with them and, as he refuses, then to remain with them and be their ruler, their savior, and lead them onward to a higher world. They plead; they tell him they have waited long for him; that he should not leave them; that he alone can save them. They cry out and appeal to him not to forsake them. This is the strongest appeal they can make. The disciple in the school of the masters holds the thought of his discipleship. By this thought he makes his decision. He knows that this world is not his world; that the forms which he sees are impermanent and decay; that the tones and voices which appeal to him are the crystallized echoes of the world's desires, which can never be satisfied. The disciple pronounces his thought to the world which has claimed him. He shows it that he knows it and will not give his word to the inner world of the senses. Immediately there is within him a sense of power with the knowledge that he has wisely judged of the sense world and refused its allurements.

His thoughts now seem to penetrate all things and to be able to change the forms of things by the very power of his thought. Matter is easily moulded by his thought. Forms give way and change into other forms by his thought. His thought enters the world of men. He sees their weaknesses and their ideals, their follies and ambitions. He sees that he can wield the minds of men by his thought; that he may stop bickerings, quarrels, contentions and strife, by his thought. He sees that he might compel warring factions to enjoy peace. He sees that he can stimulate the minds of men and open them to keener vision and to ideals higher than any they have. He sees that he may suppress or remove disease by speaking the word of health. He sees that he may take away sorrows and assume burdens of men. He sees that with his knowledge he may be a god-man among men. He sees that he may be as great or as lowly among men as he wills. The mental world seems to open and disclose its powers to him. The world of men calls him but he gives no response. Then the men struggling call in mute appeal to him. He refuses to be the ruler of men, and they ask him to be their savior. He may comfort the sorrowing, raise the lowly, enrich the poor in spirit, quiet the troubled, strengthen the weary, remove despair and enlighten the minds of men. Mankind needs him. The voices of men tell him they cannot do without him. He is necessary to their progress. He can give them the spiritual vigor which they lack and may begin a new reign of spiritual law if he will go out to men and help them. The disciple in the school of the masters dismisses the call of ambition and position. He dismisses the call to be a great teacher or a saint, though he listens well to the cry for help. The thought of his discipleship is again with him. He focusses on the calls and judges them by his one thought. Almost had he gone out to the world to help.

(To be continued)

ADEPTS, MASTERS AND MAHATMAS

(Continued)

[From *The Word*, Vol. 11 No. 2, May 1910]

THE adamantine rocks of the ages crumble. Color leaves form and forms vanish. Music goes out of sound and sounds end in wails of sadness and reproach. The fires are dead. Sap dries up. Everything is cold. The life and the light of the world are gone. All is still. Darkness prevails. The disciple in the school of the masters now enters his death period.

The inner world is dead to him; it vanishes. The outer physical world is also dead. He treads the earth, but it has the unsubstantiality of a shadow. The immovable hills are as shifting to him as the clouds and like so many veils; he sees through them into the beyond, which is emptiness. The light has gone out of the sun though it still shines. The songs of birds are as screams. All the world is seen to be in a constant state of flux and reflux; nothing is permanent, all is change. Life is a pain, though the disciple is dead to pain as to pleasure. Everything is unreal; all is a mockery. Love is a spasm. Those who seem to enjoy life are seen to be only in a delirium. The saint is self deluded, the sinner is mad. The wise are as the foolish, there is neither bad nor good. The heart of the disciple loses feeling. Time is seen to be a delusion, yet it seems to be the most real. There is no up nor down in the universe. The solid earth seems to be a dark bubble floating in darker and empty space. Though the disciple in the school of the masters walks about and physically sees things as before, the mental darkness thickens about him. Waking or sleeping, the darkness is with him. The darkness becomes a thing of horror and continually encroaches. Silence is upon him and his words seem to have no sound. The silence seems to crystallize into a formless thing which cannot be seen, and its presence is the presence of death. Go where he will, do what he will, the disciple cannot escape this dark thing. It is in everything and around everything. It is within him and around him. Annihilation were bliss as compared to the nearness of this dark thing. But for the presence of this dark thing the disciple is alone. He feels as though he is the living dead in a dead world. Though without a voice, the shapeless darkness recalls the delights of the inner world of the senses to the disciple, and when he refuses to listen he is shown that he may escape or pass out from this utter gloom if he will answer the call of men. Even while in the midst of darkness the disciple of the masters is aware that he should not heed the darkness, though he is crushed down by it. For the disciple all things have lost attraction. Ideals have disappeared. Effort is useless and there is no purpose in things. But although he is as dead the disciple is still conscious. He may struggle with the darkness, but his struggles seem useless. For the darkness eludes him while it crushes. Believing himself strong he throws himself at first against the darkness in his efforts to overcome it, only to find that it becomes heavier as he opposes it. The disciple is in the coils of the ancient serpent of the world against which human strength is as weakness. It seems to the disciple that he is in eternal death, though the life and the light have gone out of things and hold nothing for him and although his body is as his grave, yet he is still conscious. It dawns upon him that if he cannot overcome the darkness, yet the darkness has not quite overcome him, for he is conscious.

This thought of being conscious in the dark is the first glimmering of life for the disciple since he entered his death period. The disciple lies softly in the coils of death and does not fight, but remains conscious; the darkness carries on the fight. The dark neighbor urges the fight, but seeing that struggle was useless, the disciple no longer struggles. When the disciple is willing to remain perpetually in utter darkness if need be, and when he feels conscious in eternity, even though in darkness and will not yield, that thought by which things are known comes to him. He now knows that the utter gloom in which he is surrounded is his own dark faculty, a very part of his own being which is his own adversary. This thought gives him new strength, but he cannot fight, for the dark faculty is of himself though it eludes him. The disciple now trains his focus faculty to find his dark faculty. As the disciple continues to exercise his focus faculty and bring the dark faculty into range there seems to be a sundering of mind and body.

The dark faculty spreads if possible a deeper gloom. The focus faculty brings into range the disciple's thoughts of the ages. Great strength is needed by the disciple to continue the use of his focus faculty. As some old thought is thrown up from the past by the dark faculty, the disciple's attention is momentarily diverted by the thing of the past, the child of desire. Each time the disciple turns his focus faculty to bring into light the dark brother faculty, the thing of the olden time uses a new device. When seemingly within range and about to be discovered, the thing of darkness, like a devil fish, emits an impenetrable blackness which surrounds it and darkens everything. While the darkness prevails the thing again eludes the focus faculty of the disciple. As the disciple brings the focus to bear steadily into the blackness, it begins to take on form, and out of the dark gloom there come most loathsome forms. Huge worm-like creatures ooze themselves out of the blackness and around him. Giant crab-like shapes crawl out of the blackness and over him. Out of the blackness lizards waddle up and project slimy and fork-like tongues at him. Hideous creatures which were nature's failures in her early attempts to produce living things, swarm around the disciple from out of the blackness which his focus faculty makes known. They cling to him and seem to enter him and would possess his being. But the disciple continues to use his focus faculty. Out of the seemingly impenetrable darkness and in the range of the focus faculty there crawl and squirm and hover and brood things with and without form. Bats of incarnate blackness, wickedness and malice, with human or misshapen head flutter about and flap their noxious wings around him, and with the horror of their dread presence there come male and female human figures expressive of every human vice and crime. Creatures of loathsome and sickening loveliness insinuate themselves around and fasten to the disciple. Composite male and female reptilian, vermin-like human creatures beset him. But he is fearless until he discovers that they are his own creations. Then fear comes. He sickens in despair. As he looks at or feels the awful things, he sees himself reflected in each. Each looks into his heart and brain, and looks to the place it had there filled. Each cries out to him and accuses him of a past thought and action which gave it form and called it into being. All of his secret crimes through the ages rise up in the black terror before him.

Each time he ceases using his focus faculty he finds relief, but not forgetfulness. Ever he must renew his efforts and must uncover the dark faculty. Again and again he seeks out the dark faculty and as many times does it elude him. At some time, it may be in one of the darkest moments or one of relief, the one thought of the disciple comes again; and again he knows things as they are. They are the children of his past thoughts and deeds conceived in ignorance and born in darkness. He knows that they are the ghosts of his dead past, which his dark faculty has summoned and which he must transform or be borne down by. He is fearless and wills to transform them, by the one thought which he knows. He begins this, his work. Then he becomes aware of and awakens and uses his image faculty.

As soon as the disciple comes into possession of his image faculty he discovers that the dark faculty is unable to produce forms. He learns that the dark faculty had been able to throw up before him the past in forms by means of the image faculty, but as he has now taken possession of it and learns its use, the dark faculty though it still remains elusive, cannot create form. Gradually the disciple gains confidence in himself and learns to look fearlessly on his past. He marshals the events of that past in order before him. Through his image faculty he gives them the forms in which they were, and by the one thought which he knows he judges them for what they are. By the image faculty he holds the matter of his past as represented by the forms, and he returns it to the matter of the world or to the dark faculty, from either of which it came. That which is returned to the world is given direction and order and a high tone. That which is returned to the dark faculty is subdued, controlled, refined. By his image faculty the disciple is able to give form to the darkness and to image the dark faculty, but he is still unable to know the dark faculty in itself. As the disciple judges, transforms and refines his matter of the past he is able by his image faculty to inquire into the earliest forms of nature and to trace matter through its various forms from the earliest periods of involution into form, through its consecutive stages, link by link, through the entire chain of its evolutionary period to the present time. By use of his image faculty the disciple is able to trace by analogy of the past and the present the forms which will be evolved from nature and by the use of the faculties of the mind. By his image faculty and with his focus faculty he may make forms large or small. By the use of the image faculty the disciple can trace all forms to that of the mental world, but not within or beyond it. By use of the image faculty the disciple knows of the processes of the formation of present man, of his metempsychoses, transmigration and reincarnations and is able to image the processes by which he as disciple will become master of his faculties in the mental world.

The disciple may try to image to himself who he is and what is his form. But by his one thought which he knows he will know that he is as yet unborn and that though he knows of his "I" he is unable to image himself. The disciple finds that from the very first of his attempts to center the focus faculty on the dark faculty, even though it were possible, he could not have discovered the dark faculty because his attention had been diverted from it by the creatures which it made present to him. As he learns this he knows that he has stilled the dark faculty. He knows himself to be unborn, like a foetus.

Up to the present time and at the present time the disciple in the school of the masters has met with masters and knows of their presence, but only through their physical bodies. The disciple is not able to perceive a master body independently of a master's physical body and though the disciple is able to know when a master is present yet he cannot perceive distinctly of a master body; because a master body is not a sense body and cannot be perceived through the senses. And the disciple has not yet learned the use of the motive faculty independently of the senses and by its use only can a master body be known. While the disciple struggled with the dark faculty a master could not help him because the disciple was then testing his own strength, proving his steadfastness of purpose, transmuting his own matter, and to have given assistance at such time would have caused the disciple to remain mortal. But when the disciple by his own steadfastness and courage has proven himself true to his purpose and by the use of his focus and image faculties and by the one thought which he knows, has stilled the dark faculty, then the disciple is shown by a master the difficulties through which he has passed and the purpose which it has served. He finds or has shown to him that that with which he has struggled is the uncontrolled and blind desire of his human kind and that by subduing desires he aids and stimulates mankind to so act with theirs.

As yet the disciple has not overcome sleep; he has not overcome death. He knows that he cannot die, though he is in a womb of death. He no longer struggles. He awaits the maturing of time which will bring him to birth. He cannot see nor sense the processes which are passing within his physical body, though he may follow these processes in thought. But soon there comes a new movement within him. There seems to be a new influx of intelligent life. He takes mental life within his physical body, as when a foetus takes life in the womb. The disciple feels as though he might rise out of his physical body and soar where he pleases and at will. But he does not. There is a new lightness and buoyancy throughout his body and he is mentally sensitive to all things within his sphere. His thoughts will take form before him, but he knows that he should not yet give matter the form of his thought. As his time of birth approaches, the one thought which he knows is ever present with him. His focus faculty is fixed in this one thought. All things seem to blend into this thought and this one thought which he knows is through all things. He becomes more conscious of this one thought; lives in it, and while his physical body will perform its functions naturally his whole concern is in his one thought which he knows. A calm joy and peace are within him. Harmony is about him and he quickens according to his thought. Power of motion enters him. He wills to speak, but does not at once find mental voice. His effort sounds a note in the song of time. The song of time enters his being and bears him up and up. His one thought is stronger. He tries again to speak and again time responds, but he has no voice. Time seems to flood him. Power comes and his speech is born within him. As he speaks, he ascends out of the dark faculty as out of a womb. He, a master, has risen.

His speech, his voice, is his birth. It is his ascension. Never again will he pass through death. He is immortal. His speech is a word. The Word is his name. His name, his word is as the keynote of a song which is sounded throughout the time world, surrounding and permeating the physical world. His name is the theme of the song of life which is taken up and sung by every particle of time. As the harmony of time is understood, the disciple perceives himself to be a mental body. His mental body is a body of faculties, not of senses. His focus faculty he uses readily. By it he finds that he, his mental body, is the one thought by which he became a disciple in the school of the masters, the same thought which guided him through all difficulties and by which he knows things as they are; it is his motive faculty.

The master seems to have always existed. His immortality seems not to have just commenced, but to extend indefinitely into the past. He is not a physical body, he is not a psychic or astral body. He is a master body, the matter of which is thought. He thinks and time adjusts itself by his thoughts. He is in the heaven world of humanity, and finds that all humanity are there represented. He finds that though all humanity are represented in his world, the heaven world, the mental world, the world of the masters, that humanity are constantly appearing and reappearing in some new aspect. That the heaven of one is changed by that one and enjoyed differently with each reappearance and that the heaven world of anyone is changed with the changing of the ideal of that one. The master perceives that this heaven world is dimly perceived by mankind, even while they are on earth, though they fail to realize their heaven while on earth. He perceives that the heaven of mankind is made of their thoughts and that the thoughts of each build his own heaven which each realizes when the power of his mind leaves the physical body at death and is united with the ideals which are his heaven world and which he experiences between lives. The master perceives the individuals of humanity coming and going from the heaven world, each extending or limiting the period of his experience according to his ideal and according to the motive by which he learns from his experience and the causes of his experiencing. The master perceives that the mind of the personality of a life thinks of itself in connection with the highest thoughts, as its personality, but does not realize the different periods of incarnation while in the heaven world. But the master does not yet follow the minds in their coming and going from the heaven world.

The master sees in the heaven world that those who come and enter it after death and were by their ideals represented in it during physical life, do not know of the heaven world as he knows it. The unborn men yet resting in the heaven world, enjoy heaven as they had known of it in their physical lives. Though there are beings who live consciously and throughout time in the heaven world, yet mortal men resting in this heaven world do not know these beings, and during their stay they are unaware of the presence of masters, unless the thought of masters had been part of their ideals in physical life. The master sees that in the heaven world man is a thought body, stripped of his physical body; that man's heaven is a transitory state though a state more real to him than was his physical life; that as a thought body without his physical body, man uses his image faculty and thereby constructs his heaven-world; that the kind of a man's heaven world is decided by the motive of the mind who made it.

Of all this the master had known while he was a disciple; now it is known by him. The heaven world which is to the mind of a mortal an immense expanse of years, is, to a master, a brief dream only. Time in the mental world when conceived by the mind of a mortal is endless eternity as compared with the time of the physical world. The mortal in his heaven state cannot use his time faculty; the master does. The time faculty of the master is brought into use, by his motive faculty, as he thinks. As he thinks, the atoms of time group themselves and are related to each other as his thought, and that is determined and caused by his motive. The master thinks of time, its comings and goings. He follows time and sees the circulations from the beginnings of time, its constant flow from the spiritual world, its flooding and turning back into the spiritual world. The motive causes its comings and decides its goings, in periods necessary for the realization and working out of its ideals.

The master thinks of his motive and his motive faculty makes known to him the motive which prompted his becoming a master. While he seems to have always been a master, he knows that his becoming one is the fullness of his time. The beginnings of this, though far removed in the lower time worlds are present in the mental world, his world. He knows that the completion of his beginning is his becoming, and its uniting with the beginning. But he knows that the processes of the becoming are not here; they are in the lower time worlds.

Other motives than the motive which caused him to become what he is, are made known to him as he thinks and uses his motive faculty. He has followed time in its beginnings and in its completions, but he does not see all the processes of his becoming a master. He thinks of the processes and uses his image and focus faculties. The flowing of time continues. He follows it in its groupings and formation of the worlds. The worlds take on form as form-time, which is form-matter, and forms appear upon them. The atoms of time fill in the forms, which are the time molecules. The atoms of time pass through the form molecules; they pass through the form world, and while they are flowing on the forms become physical. The physical world, as the form world made visible and concrete, is seen to be a constant flowing on of time and not to be concrete and solid. Forms appear and disappear like bubbles, and time which flows on continues through the forms which are thrown up on it and borne away on it. These throwings up and drawings in are the lives and deaths of things which come into the physical world. The human forms are among them. He sees a continuous line of forms, graduated in perspective, stretching over the bounds of the physical world and ending in himself. These forms or bubbles lead into himself. By his focus faculty he lines them up and sees that they are the forms or the shadows of himself. He focusses them, and all end now and blend into and disappear in the physical body, his present physical body, from which he has but just risen, ascended as a master.

He is immortal; his immortality is the whole of time. Though the whole becoming has extended throughout time, it has been lived through while he has taken voice and given name to himself, and during his ascension. His physical body is in the same position and, according to physical time, not many moments seem to have lapsed.

The master now is in full possession of his physical organs; he is aware of the physical world; he is in full possession of five of his mental faculties and uses them independently of his senses. His physical body rests; peace is upon it; he is transfigured. He, the master, as a master body, is not of the form of the physical body. He is in the physical, but he extends beyond it. The master is aware of and sees other masters about him. They speak to him as one of them.

The disciple who was and who has now become a master, lives and acts consciously in the physical and mental worlds. His physical body is within the master body, as the physical world is within and permeated by the mental world. Through or by use of the physical body the physical world is alive to him. Everything in the physical world is more pronounced. The sun shines, birds sing, the waters pour forth their melody of joy, and manifested nature greets the master as her creator and preserver. The world of the inner senses which beckoned him as disciple now gladly offers obedience and submissive service to the master. That to which he did not yield as disciple he now will guide and direct as master. He sees that to the world of men, which had offered him glory and had asked his aid, he may now render service and he will give it aid. He regards his physical body with sympathy and compassion. He looks on it as the thing through which he has come into his own.

(To be continued)

ADEPTS, MASTERS AND MAHATMAS

(Continued)

[From *The Word,* Vol. 11 No. 3, June 1910]

THE master enquires concerning the processes by which he has become what he is, and reviews the terrors which had beset him in the darkness in which he was immersed while a disciple. There is no pang of suffering now. Fear is gone. The darkness has no terrors for him, for darkness is subdued though not completely changed.

As the master reviews the transformations of his becoming, he perceives the thing which was the cause of all past hardships and heart stifling gloom, and above which he has risen, but from which he is not quite separated. That thing is the old elusive, formless darkness of desire, from which and out of which came myriad forms and formless dread. That formless thing is at last formed.

Here it lies now, a sphinx-like form asleep. It waits to be called to life by him if he will speak the word of life for it. It is the sphinx of the ages. It is like a half human beast which can fly; but now it rests. It is asleep. This is the thing which guards the Path and allows no one to pass who does not conquer it.

The sphinx calmly gazes on, while man dwells in the coolness of groves, while he throngs the market place, or makes his abode in pleasing pastures. However, to the explorer of life, to him to whom the world is a desert and who boldly tries to pass over its wastes into the beyond, to him the sphinx propounds her riddle, nature's riddle, which is the problem of time. Man answers it when he becomes immortal—an immortal man. He who cannot give answer, he who does not master desire, to him the sphinx is a monster, and it devours him. He who solves the problem, masters death, conquers time, subdues nature and he goes over her subdued body along his path.

This the master has done. He has outgrown physical life, though he remains still in it; he has conquered death, though he may still have to take on bodies which will die. He is a master of time, though in time, and he is a worker with its laws. The master sees that at the birth from his physical body, which was his ascension, he had in passing freed the sphinx body from his physical body, and to that which was formless he has given form; that in this form are represented the energies and capacities of all animal bodies in physical life. The sphinx is not physical. It has the strength and courage of the lion, and is animal; it has the freedom of the bird, and the intelligence of the human. It is the form in which all the senses are and in which they may be used in their fullness.

The master is in the physical and mental worlds, but not in the astral-desire world; he has silenced it by subduing the sphinx body. To live and act in the astral world also, he must call into action his sphinx body, his desire body, which now sleeps. He calls; he speaks the word of power. It arises from its rest and stands beside his physical body. It is in form and feature the same as his physical body. It is human in form, and of exceeding strength and beauty. It rises to the call of its master and answers. It is the adept body, an adept.

With the coming to life and into action of the adept body, the inner sense world, the astral world, is sensed and seen and known, as when returning to his physical body the master again knows the physical world. The adept body sees his physical body and may enter it. The master is through them both, but is not the form of either. The physical body is aware of the adept within, though it cannot see him. The adept is aware of the master who has called him into action and whom he obeys, but whom he cannot see. He knows his master as an ordinary man knows but cannot see his conscience. The master is with them both. He is the master in the three worlds. The physical body acts as a physical man in the physical, but it is ordered and directed by the adept who is now its ruler. The adept acts in the astral world, the inner world of the senses; but though having free action, he acts in accord with the master's will, because he feels the master's presence, is aware of his knowledge and power, and knows it is best to be guided by the mind of the master rather than by influence of his senses. The master acts in his own world, the mental world, which includes the astral and physical worlds.

To man acting in the physical world, it seems strange, if not impossible, that he should have three bodies or be developed into three bodies, which may act separately from and independent of each other. To man in his present state it is impossible; yet, as man, he has these three as principles or potential bodies which are now blended and undeveloped, and without either of which he would not be man. His physical body gives man a place in the physical world. His desire principle gives him force and action in the physical world, as man. His mind gives him the power of thought and reason. Each of these is distinct. When one leaves, the others are incapacitated. When all act together man is a power in the world. In his unborn state man can have neither his physical body, nor his desire, nor his mind, act intelligently and independently of the other two, and, because he does not know himself apart from his body and his desire, it seems strange that he, as a mind, could act independently and intelligently apart from his desire and his physical body.

As has been stated in the preceding articles, man may develop either his desire or his mind, so that either will act intelligently and act independently of his physical body. What is now the animal in man may be trained and developed by the mind who acts with and in it, so that it will become an entity independent of the physical body. The development or birth of the desires into a body in which the mind acts and serves, similarly as the mind of man now serves his physical body, is that of an adept. An adept does not usually destroy or leave his physical body; he uses it to act in the physical world, and though he may act independently of his physical body and move freely even when away from it, yet, it is his own form. But the desire body of man is merely a principle and is without form during his life.

It may seem strange that man's desire may be developed into form and given birth, and that that desire form may act separately from his physical body, and that similarly his mind may act as a distinct body independently of either. Yet it is no more strange than that a woman should give birth to a boy who is in appearance and tendencies different from her own nature and that of the father.

Flesh is born of flesh; desire is born of desire; thought is born of the mind; each body is born from its own nature. Birth comes after conception and maturity of body. That which the mind is able to conceive it is possible for it to become.

The physical body of man is like a man asleep. Desire does not act through it; mind does not act through it; it cannot act of itself. If a building is on fire and the fire scorches, the flesh does not feel it, but when the burning reaches the nerves it awakens the desire and calls it into action. Desire acting through the senses causes the physical body to beat down women and children, if they stand in its way of escape to a place of safety. But if, while on the way, the cry of a wife or child should reach into the heart and the man rushes to their rescue and risks his life to save them, this is the mental man, who overcomes the maddened desire and guides its power, so that through the physical body it lends its efforts at rescue. Each of the men is distinct from the other, yet all act together.

That an adept, being of the same form as his physical body should enter and act through his physical body is no more strange than that the white blood cells of the body should pass through other cells or the connective tissues of the body, yet they do. It is no more strange than that some semi-intelligence which is the control of a medium should act in the medium's body or emerge from it as a distinct and separate form; yet the truth of such occurrence has been attested by some able men of science.

Things which are strange should not be therefore ignored. Statements which are strange should be taken for what they are worth; it is not wise to speak of what one does not understand, as being ridiculous or impossible. It may be called ridiculous by one who has looked at it from all sides and without prejudice. He who discards as ridiculous an important statement without having used his reason is not making use of his prerogative as a man.

One who becomes a master does not bend the efforts of his mind to become an adept by developing his desire body. He turns all effort to the overcoming and subduing of his desire and developing as distinct the entity of his mind. It has been explained that one who becomes a master does not first become an adept. The reason is that by becoming an adept the mind is bound more securely to the desires than while in the physical body; for the desire body, as an adept, acting in the inner and astral world of the senses has there more power over the mind than has the unformed desire body, while the mind of man acts in his body in the physical world. But when man has bent all efforts toward entering the mental world consciously and intelligently, and after he has so entered, he does by the power of mind that which is done by the aspirant to adeptship, by the power of desire. One who becomes a master becomes first aware of and lives consciously in the mental world, and then descends to the inner sense world of the adepts, which then has no power over him. The unborn mind of the adept has an unequal struggle with the fully developed desire body which is the adept, and so a man who becomes first an adept is not likely to become a master in that period of evolution.

This applies to the races of men as they now are. In earlier times and before desire had gained such ascendency over the minds of men, the natural way of development after incarnation into physical bodies was, that the desire body was developed and born through and from the physical body. Then the mind could, through its efforts at management of its desire body be born through its adept desire body, as that was born through its physical body. As the races of men developed further and the minds were more dominated by desire those who became adepts remained adepts and did not or could not become masters. With the birth of the Aryan race, the difficulties were increased. The Aryan race has desire as its dominant principle and force. This desire controls the mind which is developing through it.

Mind is the matter, the thing, the power, the principle, the entity, which is developing through all other races, from the earliest periods of the manifested worlds. Mind in its development, passes through the races, and is developed through the races.

The physical body is the fourth race, represented in the zodiac by libra ♎, sex, and the only race which is visible to man, though all the other preceding races are present inside and about the physical. Desire is the fifth race, represented in the zodiac by the sign scorpio ♏, desire, which is striving to take on form through the physical. This fifth, desire race, should have been controlled by the mind in earlier periods and especially while operating those physical bodies usually called the Aryan race. But as the mind has not dominated and controlled desire and as it has and is becoming stronger, desire overcomes and attaches the mind to itself, so that it now has the ascendency. Therefore, the mind of a man who works for adeptship is held captive in the adept body, even as man's mind is now held captive in the prison house of his physical body. The fifth race, if developed naturally to its fulness, would be a race of adepts. The incarnate mind of man acting freely, and being fully developed, is or will be the sixth race, and is shown in the zodiac by the sign sagittary ♐, thought. The sixth race began in the middle of the fifth race as the fifth race began in the middle of the fourth race, and as the fourth race began in the middle of the third race.[1]

The fifth race is not fully developed, because desire acting through man is not developed. The only representatives of the

---

[1] This figure will be shown in the July issue of THE WORD [*p. 175 in this book*].

fifth race are adepts, and they are not physical but are fully developed desire bodies. The sixth race will be thought bodies, not physical bodies nor desire (adept) bodies. The sixth race when fully developed will be a race of masters and that race is now represented by the masters. The master's work is to aid the incarnate minds of men to reach up by effort to their attainment in the mental world, which is their native world. The Ayran race, which is a physical race, has more than half run its course.

There is no exact line of demarcation where one race ends or another race begins, yet there are distinct markings according to the lives of men. Such markings are made by events in the lives of men and are at or about the time of such changes recorded in the writings as history or marked by records in stone.

The discovery of America and the landing of the Pilgrims marked the beginning of the formation of the sixth great race. Each great race develops on its own continent and spreads out into branches over all the world. The landing of the Pilgrims was a physical landing, but it marked the beginnings of a new era in the development of the mind. The characteristic and dominant feature of the sixth race, which began in America and is now developing in and through the United States, is thought. Thought characterizes the race which is forming in the United States, as desire is the dominant feature of the fifth race which was born in Asia, spread over the world and is wearing out in Europe.

The types of thought of the thought race will give different features and physical types to the fourth race bodies of the sixth or thought race, which will be as distinct in their way as a Mongolian body is from a Caucasian. The races have their seasons and run their courses as naturally and according to law, as one season is followed by another. But those among a race who so will, need not die with their race. A race decays, a race dies, because it does not attain its possibilities. Those of a race who will, by individual effort, may attain what would be possible to the race. Hence one may develop to be an adept because he has the force of the race behind him. One may become a master because he has the power of thought. Without desire, one could not be an adept; with it, he can. Without the power to think one cannot become a master; by thought, he can.

Because the mind is working in the desire world and with desires; because desire has dominance over mind; because the time has passed for man to try by natural development to become an adept, he should not try for adeptship first. Because man cannot likely grow out of adeptship and become a master; because the new race is one of thought; because he may with safety to himself and others develop by thought and because he can be of more service to himself and his race by attaining the possibilities of his race, it is better for him who seeks progress or attainment to place himself in thought with and seek entrance in the school of the masters, and not in the school of the adepts. To try for adeptship now, is like planting grain in late summer. It will take root and it will grow but will not come to perfection and may be killed or stunted by the frosts. When planted at the proper season in the spring it develops naturally and will come to full growth. Desire acts on the mind as do the frosts on unripe grain, which they wither in its husk.

When man becomes a master he has passed through all that the adept passes through but not in the way in which the adept develops. The adept develops through his senses. The mind develops as master through his mind faculties. The senses are comprehended in the faculties. That which a man goes through in becoming an adept, and what he experiences in the sense world through his desires, the disciple of the masters passes through mentally, overcoming the desires by the mind. In the overcoming of the desires by the mind, desire is given form, because thought gives form to desire; desire must take form according to thought if the thought will not take form in desire. So that when the master by his faculties reviews the processes of his becoming from discipleship, he finds desire has taken form and that the form awaits his call to action.

(To be continued)

ADEPTS, MASTERS AND MAHATMAS

(Continued)

[From *The Word,* Vol. 11 No. 4, July 1910]

FIGURE 33 is here given to show the nature of each of the races which contribute to the making of man, how and under what dominant character and sign each race begins and is developed and ends, and how each race is related to and affected by those which precede or which follow it. A few suggestions will indicate some of that which may be found in this symbol.

The Figure 33 shows the great zodiac with seven smaller zodiacs. Each of the seven surrounds one of the seven lower signs of the great zodiac. Within the lower half of the great zodiac are drawn lesser zodiacs, one within the other, in the proportions heretofore given in figure 30, and symbolizing respectively the physical man and the physical world, the psychic man and the psychic world, the mental man and the mental world and the spiritual man and the spiritual world.

The horizontal diameter from ♋ to ♑ of the great zodiac is the line of manifestation; above is that which is unmanifested, below is the manifested universe. In this figure are shown seven races on four planes, the planes being the spiritual plane which begins with ♋ and ends with ♑, the mental plane which begins with ♌ and ends with ♐, the psychic plane begins with ♍ and ends with ♏, and the physical plane of ♎, which is the pivotal plane for the upper three planes in their involutionary and evolutionary aspects.

The vertical diameter, from ♈ to ♎, symbolizes consciousness; this extends throughout the unmanifested and the manifested. These two lines, the vertical and horizontal, apply in the sense here used to the great zodiac; not to the seven lesser zodiacs representing here the seven races. In the fourth race, the race of ♎, the line symbolizing consciousness is vertical, as to the horizontal diameter of the great circle, and identical and coincident in part with the line symbolizing consciousness in the great zodiac. This is not a matter of accident.

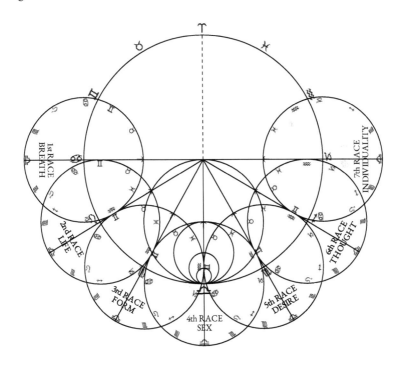

FIGURE 33

The lower half of the great circle symbolizes the horizontal diameter or line of manifestation of the seven races unfolded, involving and evolving. From the center, the point at which matter (that is, spirit-matter, the dual manifestation of substance) becomes conscious, radiate seven lines which, extended, coincide in part with the diameters of the seven lesser zodiacs. These vertical diameters, each from ♈ to ♎ in the lesser circles, symbolize the line along which each race develops consciously. The horizontal diameter in each zodiac of the seven from ♋ to ♑, is a curved line, coincident, in figure 33, with the periphery of the great zodiac.

Each race begins its development at the sign ♋ in its own zodiac, reaches its middle point at ♎ and ends at ♑.

The second race began at the middle or ♎ of the first race and at ♋ of its own zodiac, and ended at ♑ of its own zodiac and in the middle of the third race, which was the beginning of the fourth race. The third race began at the end of the first, the middle of the second and ended at the middle of the fourth race, which was the beginning of the fifth race. The fourth race began at the end of the second race, which was the middle of the third race, and ends at the middle of the fifth race, which was the beginning of the sixth race. The fifth race began at the end of the third race, which was the middle of the fourth race, and will end at the middle of the sixth race, which will be the beginning of the seventh race. The sixth race began at the end of development of the fourth race which was the middle of the fifth race, and it will end at the middle of the seventh race.

The first race began with the beginning of the universe, which came out from the unmanifested. The first race began at its sign ♋ and became consciousness only at its middle period, when it reached its ♎︎, which was the beginning of its line of consciousness. The line of its consciousness was and is also the line of manifestation of the great zodiac. The first race has not ended. It does not die throughout the period of manifestation.

The development of the seventh race will begin at the end of the fifth race which is the middle of the sixth race and will be completed in its sign of ♑︎, which will be in the unmanifested. Its line of consciousness completes the line of manifestation of the great zodiac. More could be written in elucidation of Figure 33, but the foregoing is sufficient to explain the symbolism relating to the matter here treated.

There is a great difference between one who becomes an adept before he becomes a master and the adept who is born after his master. The difference is that the first kind of adept has an unborn mind, whereas, the master, the mind, has a fully developed adept. The adept of the master can at all times act in accordance with the laws of the mental world, because the master, acts through him and he responds to thought more readily than the brain responds to the action of the mind. The adept whose mind is unborn, acts under the laws of the desire world, but he cannot or does not know clearly the law above him, around him, which is the law of time, the law of the mental world. He cannot control it nor can he act in perfect accordance with it. He acts according to the law of the astral world, the world of the inner senses, which world is a reflection and reaction from the physical world and from the mental world. The adept with his unborn mind will most likely remain unborn in the mental world at the close of the manifestation of the cycle of worlds. The adept of the master has been raised and born legitimately of the mind, and his heritage will be the mental world into which he will pass after the master has become a mahatma.

The adept with the unborn mind does not have the independent use of the mental faculties, though these faculties are used by him in a greater or more pronounced degree than the intelligent man of the world is able to use them. The independent and intelligent use of the mental faculties belongs exclusively to the disciple of the masters, who learns to use them fully only when he becomes a master.

The independent and intelligent use of the focus faculty causes the self appointed disciple to become and constitutes him an accepted disciple in the school of the masters. The free use of the image and dark faculties belongs to the adept who is made adept by his master. The free use of the time and motive faculties is had by the master only. But the master cannot fully and freely use the light and the I-am faculties, though he knows of them and they act through his other faculties. The free use of the light and I-am faculties is had by the mahatma only.

The master has full possession of and uses his time and image and focus and dark and motive faculties, independently of the inner senses, such as sight, hearing, taste, smell, touch, moral and I senses, or their action into the physical world. Instead of a dreary waste or a world of darkness and confusion, the master knows that the physical world is a place where heaven may reign. He sees the physical world to be more beautiful than eye can see, a place where harmonies prevail that the ear cannot detect, and where forms are grander than the mind of man can imagine. He sees it as the place of change and trial where all beings may be purified, where death must be overcome by all in turn, where man will be able to know and discriminate the true from the false, and where he will some day walk as the lord and master of his forms, the conqueror of illusion, while he still uses it for those beings who are nursed through it into the real.

From the mental world, the heaven world, the master acts through the inner world of the senses into the physical world and while using the inner senses and the physical body he controls them by his faculties. By his mental faculties through his senses and in his physical body, he can interpret the illusion of matter in the three worlds of its transformations. By means of his focus faculty he can bring into the physical world and make present there the thoughts of the mental and forms of the astral worlds. He can perceive the astral and mental through the physical. He sees the harmonies and beauties of the combinations of the physical, astral and mental. Through his time faculty the master can hear and see the atoms of time as they constantly flow through the physical matter and on, and he knows the measure and duration of a form made physical, because he knows the tone to which it is set and sounds. By this tone which is the time limit and measure, he knows the period the form will last until the physical matter in the form is borne on and into the time world from which it came. By his image faculty the master can create a form and cause it to be made visible by the flowing into and through it of the units of time, the time atoms. Through the image faculty he can cause forms to appear infinitely great or infinitely small. He may magnify or enlarge a molecule to the size of the world, or cause a world to appear as small as a molecule. This he does by holding the form in his image faculty and increasing or reducing its size by means of his focus faculty.

By means of his focus faculty the master enters or leaves the physical and psychic worlds or any portions of them. By means of the focus faculty, he relates and adjusts the faculties to each other and to the senses through which the faculties may act.

By means of the dark faculty he can cause to disappear or to be transformed any of the forms which he has called into existence. Through the dark faculty he can produce sleep in any being that breathes. By exercise of the dark faculty the master may prevent the minds of men from entering the realms of the mental world before their time, and he sometimes does it when an entrance would cause their becoming unbalanced, or he may give them power to subject other minds to their own and he does it to check men who train their minds with the object of controlling others. By exercise of the dark faculty, on a man's mind he may cause the man to be confused, bewildered, and forgetful of the object he had in view. By means of the dark faculty a master may befog the senses and prevent curious and inquisitive people from discovering that to which they have no right. By exercise of the dark faculty the master checks the inquisitive from sensing, reading or knowing the thoughts of others. By means of the dark faculty the master prevents those who seek for selfish ends, from learning of words and their power.

By use of his motive faculty the master knows the motives of men which prompt them to action. The master knows by the motive faculty that man's motives are the mainsprings of his life and that they, though often unknown to man, are the causes of all occurrences of importance in his life. Through his motive faculty he knows that motives are the causes of thought, which creates all things in the three manifested worlds. Through the motive faculty the master knows the kinds and classes and degrees of all thoughts of which men are capable, and of thoughts as beings of the mental world. Through the motive faculty he knows of the nature of his own master body and of his own motive by which it has come into fullness. By his motive faculty he can follow the trains of thought which have been worked out in the coming into fullness of his time in the mental world. Through his motive faculty he looks into the other motives which he might have but did not act from. By comparison of his motive with other motives he may judge and does judge his own motive, which is the cause of his action in the three worlds. Through his motive he knows what is and so chooses his work as a master. Through his motive faculty he knows that his work is not yet done, if he would pass into the spiritual world as a mahatma. By his motive faculty he knows that he has outgrown life, overcome death, that he is immortal and has worked out the karma of the life of the body through which he has attained, but that he has not completely exhausted the karma of each and of all the personalities through which the mind has incarnated, or else that he has obligations, duties, of which he could not acquit himself in the present life because those others to whom he owes a debt or is obligated are not in human form. He knows that even though he may have worked out all his own karma, exhausted the karma of all his lives, it may still be necessary for him to take another human form or many human forms, as a duty to which he may have pledged himself to the world and as decided by the motives which caused the taking of his pledge. By his motive faculty the master knows the causes which have determined his work.

By the time faculty he will know of the periods and appearances and the cycles of his own work and, of the periods of those with whom and for whom he will work. By his image faculty, he may know the forms in which they will appear. He knows that his own form and features will be about as they now are in physical outline. By the dark faculty he will know how and under what conditions the forms or races with whom he will work, shall die or be changed. By the focus faculty he will know where those are for and with whom he will act and the conditions under which they will appear.

The mental faculties of the master do not act separately nor entirely independently of each other. Similarly to the senses of man they act in combination or relation to each other. As a man may anticipate the taste of a lemon by hearing its name, or by its odor, or by touching it, so a master would know the nature and duration of a form through his motive faculty, and would find any of the transformations of that form by use of his focus faculty.

So the master carries on his work and assists in the completions of the cycles of time. When his physical body is worn out and he needs another, he takes it from the early and pure stock of humanity previously mentioned. If his work leads him among men he appears usually as an unknown and obscure person and does his work as quietly and inconspicuously as the requirements will permit. Men who see him see his physical body only. They cannot see him as a master body, though they may see his physical body, which gives evidence of the presence of the adept within it, and the master around it and through it, by the quiet power which it carries, the benign influence which it imparts, the love which it engenders and the simple wisdom in his words.

A master does not often come among mankind because it is not well for men. It is not well for men, because the presence of a master about and through his physical body prematurely quickens men. The presence of a master is like one's own conscience. A master's physical presence quickens the conscience in man and causes him to be aware of his shortcomings, vices and untruthfulness, and, although it also wakens all of the good qualities and encourages the virtues in him, yet man's knowledge of his virtues, side by side with his being conscious of his evil tendencies and untruthfulness, brings almost overwhelming remorse and regrets, which sap his strength and make his path seem hopelessly dark with insurmountable obstacles. This is more than his egotism can stand and he withers under the influence which were he more mature would quicken and assist him. The presence of a master does not make the fight in man's nature unequal; it causes the nature and its qualities to become manifest and apparent. This is so not by the will of the master, but because of his presence. His presence gives life to the inner nature and tendencies and makes them apparent, as sunlight makes visible all forms on the earth. Sunlight does not will the trees to bear fruit, birds to sing, nor flowers to bloom. Trees bear fruit, birds sing, and flowers bloom and each species manifests itself according to its nature because of the sun's presence, not because the sun wills that they should. The sun increases in strength as winter is passed and the season of spring advances. The gradual advance and increasing strength of the sun is borne by the tender plants as they shoot out upward in response to the warmth. They cannot stand and flourish under the sun's strength, until they are fully grown. Were the sun to shine suddenly and continuously on the young plants they would be withered by its strength. So it is with big and little men of the world who, like young plants, are unable to grow under the powerful influence of a master. Therefore a master does not come among men in his physical body, if the needs of the time will permit being cared for by a disciple of the masters. The influence of the masters is in the world at all times and surrounds it; but this influence affects the minds of men only who are susceptible to it. Their physical bodies and their desires are not in touch with the influence, and therefore do not feel it. Not the bodies, but the minds only of men can be affected by the masters.

Removed from the world of ordinary men, the master still is aware of and acts upon it; but he acts through the minds of men. The master does not consider men as they consider themselves. Men in the world are known to the master in his mental world when and as they are there represented by their thoughts and ideals. A master knows a man by his motive. When a man's motive is right he assists him in his thoughts toward the attainment of his ideal, and though men may say that they are promoted by right motives and have unselfish ideals, they cannot know because they do not know their motives and, therefore, cannot judge their ideals. A master is not affected by whims nor sentiments. These do not appear in the mental world as thoughts or ideals. Whims and sentiments and idle wishes never reach the mental world; they remain in the emotional astral desire world and are moved or blown about by the impulses as heavy smoke is blown about or shifted by gusts of wind. When a man has worked earnestly and assiduously and with devotion to his ideal, and his motive shows that he is entitled to it, the master thinks and his thought reaches the mind of the assiduous devotee who then sees the way of attainment of his ideal. This seeing comes after effort, and there is a mental joy and happiness which follows it. Then the man who had strained and struggled sets himself about his work confidently and with assurance and because he sees the way in which it is to be done. In this way a master may and does help man. But a master does not assist man by proclamations, nor by sending messages or issuing edicts, because a master wants men to use their reason as their authority for action, and not to take as authority the word of another. Those who issue edicts, send messages and make pronouncements, are not masters. At least they are not masters as are here described. A master may cause a message to be given to the world, but the message must be taken on its own merits, on the nature of the message and the principle involved. To say that a message is from a master will cause the believer to accept it without judgment, and will cause the unbeliever to ridicule its pretended source. In either case the message will fail in its purpose. But if the message is given inconspicuously without pride or pretense by the channel through whom it comes and on its own merit, the reasoning unbeliever will accept it without prejudice and the believer will take it because it will appeal to him with power and because it is right.

With an accepted disciple in the school of the masters, a master acts through the one thought by which he becomes consciously an accepted disciple. The master speaks to men through their ideals. He speaks to the disciple through thought. He speaks to other masters by motive and by his presence.

Though a master has not a human form, his form is quite as individual as that of a physical man. Were it possible for human eyes to see the forms of masters, they would, though all the same in principle, seem less alike than those who are daily met on busy streets.

For a man of the street, or a man of action, there is a great deal to be done. He is busy, and others of his kind are busy, and all must hurry. To the busy man, a master without human form, without senses, with mental faculties only, living in the mental world where night and day do not exist, where there is nothing of the senses present, to the busy man, such a picture would be inane, flat, perhaps less interesting than a picture of a sense-heaven where angels flutter over rivers of milk and honey or pass lightly over jasper streets and float around the great white throne.

The man of hurry cannot be blamed if he thinks such description flat. But ideals toward the masters will not always be flat, even to the busy man. Some day the claws of his desires will scratch and awaken him, or his mental growth may reach upward beyond his desires and his busy play in life, and then on his mental horizon there will come a thought he had not before had, and he will awaken to the ideal of the mind. This ideal will not leave him. He will continue to dream of his ideal and the dream will become gradually a waking dream and, at some day, most likely in a future life, the waking dream will become reality to him; then what was reality will be a dream, a dream of the childhood of his lives from which he has passed, as the days of children pass when they become men. He will then look back on the busy life of his childhood, with its momentous questions, with its burdens and responsibilities, its duties, sorrows and its joys. He will then look back on it as another busy man looks back on his early childhood with its important play, with its serious lessons, its merry laughter, bitter tears, and all of the wonderful exploits and things which make a child's atmosphere and world and shut it in from those who are older than it.

Masters are engaged with the ideals and the thoughts of men, as parents are with the play of their little ones. Like the prudent mother or kind father who look on at the play of their little ones and listen patiently to their dreams, so the masters look on at the little ones in the nursery, and in the school of life. Masters are more patient than parents, because they have no ill temper; they are not peevish nor dyspeptic, and can listen and understand as parents never can. The busy man has no time to learn to think, and he does not think. A master always does. Masters have much to do and do much and do all that they have to do. But it is a different work than that of the busy man.

The masters are the elder men of the race. Without them there would be no progress for man, because men, like children, if left to themselves before their maturity, will die in childhood or else revert to the animal state and condition. As children are drawn out and acquainted with life by their elders, so masters lead on and draw upward the minds of men.

As men approach their ideals and are ready for higher ideals, the masters direct their minds to the eternal verities, here called ideas, in the spiritual world. Their thought of an idea is the ideal held in the mental world by the master, and the minds of the leaders of men in the world of men, who are ready, catch glimpses of the ideal and by their thoughts bring it into their world of men. As the leaders of men speak the thought, the new ideal, into the world of men, those who listen to them are impressed by the thought; they take it up and look up to it as their ideal. In this way man is ever led on and educated by his ideals if he will only think upward rather than downward. In this way, by giving to men new ideals as teachers give their scholars new lessons, mankind is led onward in its growth by the masters who, though not seen, are ever present.

According to the ideals of humanity as a whole or the race in part or a few leaders, the masters think, and time arranges itself and flows according to their thought. The power of the masters is their thought. Their thought is their speech. They think, they speak, and the time flows on, bringing into fullness the aspirations of man. The word of the masters keeps the world in balance. The word of the masters keeps it in its form. The masters' word causes the revolution of the world. But though the masters' word sounds through and supports the world, few ears can hear its tone, few eyes can see its form, few minds can comprehend its meaning. Yet all minds are trying to understand the meaning of the age, which the masters' word has spoken into being. Many eyes look forward to see what it will bring, and ears are strained to catch the note, which the new age sounds.

From age to age in the time world, in the mental world, in the heaven world of man, the master works until he works out all measures of time. His cycle of necessary incarnations ended, his physical, psychic and mental karma long since exhausted, with his physical and adept desire bodies in their respective worlds acting with and for the law, the master thus acting from the mental world is ready to become a mahatma, to enter the spiritual world.

The passing of a master as mahatma into the spiritual world is not attended by the difficulties nor preceded by the darkness that attend the birth of the disciple through its womb of darkness into the day of the mental world. The master knows the way, and knows how to enter the spiritual world. But he does not enter before the measures of time are run. Standing in his physical body and through his adept body, the master speaks the word of birth. By his word of birth he is born. By his word of birth the master's name passes into or becomes one with his name as mahatma. The word of his birth as mahatma is called into being by the use of his light faculty and his I-am faculty. As he gives his name by these faculties, he enters the spiritual world. There he has always been, but could not perceive it, could not realize it, until the use of the light and the I-am faculties realized it.

In becoming a mahatma all faculties are blended into one being. All faculties become the I-am. I-am is the mahatma. I-am no longer thinks, for thinking ends with knowledge. The mahatma, I-am, knows. He is knowledge. As mahatma, no one faculty acts alone. All are together as one, and all are the end of all thinking. They are knowledge.

To the mahatma, the physical, buzzing world has disappeared. The inner desire world of sensation is stilled. All thought in the mental world has stopped. The three manifested worlds of time have disappeared into and blended with the spiritual world. The worlds have gone, but they are comprehended in the spiritual world by the mahatma. In the worlds of time, which were made up of indivisible particles which are the ultimate divisions of time, each world was distinct in itself, but at the fulling of time, when time runs into its sources from the mental world, all the individual units run together like drops of water, and are blended, and all make up the eternity, the spiritual world which is one.

He who has entered and knows eternity is the eternity. He knows that he was and is ever and always I-am. All things are present in this knowledge. As I-am knows itself, limitless light abounds, and though there are no eyes to see it, the light knows itself. I-am knows itself as light, and light is I-am. If the mahatma wills to be throughout eternity only as he knows himself, I-am, as being, he shuts out from his light the manifested worlds, and remains I-am, his light, the light throughout the eternity. In the ancient eastern philosophies, this state is spoken of as entrance into nirvana.

The becoming of mahatma and such entrance into nirvana is not determined at the time or after he becomes a mahatma; it is decided by a master through his motive faculty, and that decision or the causes of such decision have been determined by and made up of all the motives which have prompted man in his efforts in overcoming and toward attainment. This choice is that of those ascetics who do not love the world, and leave it that they may attain their own deserved bliss. The choice results from the beginnings of man as he sees and thinks of himself as distinct and separate from others and does not relate himself to others.

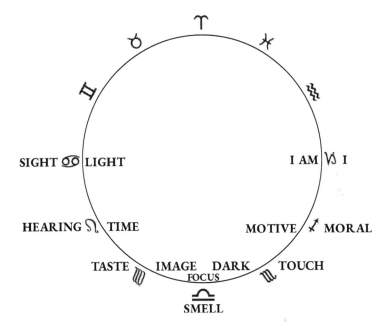

FIGURE 34
*The Faculties of the Mind and the Senses
Which Correspond to Them*

The master who thinks of the welfare of mankind for the sake of mankind, and not that he shall advance, does not on becoming mahatma remain in the quiet bliss of nirvana. The mahatma who remains in his bliss knows I-am, as I only. He who knows beyond and within the I, knows I-am, as I; but he also knows I-am, as Thou. He does not remain in the knowledge of his own light. He speaks the knowledge of his light, which is the light, into the three manifested worlds. When one on becoming mahatma speaks his light, all the worlds respond and receive new power, and the unselfish love is felt through all beings. One who has grown into the one light, one who knows the spiritual identity of all beings, will always speak into the world the light which he has become. The light thus given lives in the world and cannot die, and though it may not be seen by men, still it will shine, and the hearts of men to whom it is spoken will find it at the ripening of their time.

The mahatma who has chosen to remain as an eternal light through the manifested worlds retains his physical, adept and master bodies. One cannot become a mahatma without his physical body, but not every mahatma keeps his physical body. The physical body is necessary for the development and birth of all bodies. The physical body is that in which spiritual and mental and psychic and physical matter is transmuted, balanced and evolved. The physical body is the pivot of the worlds.

The mahatma who remains through the worlds and in the worlds uses the faculties which relate to the worlds on which he acts. But a mahatma uses the faculties differently from a master. A master uses his faculties by thought, a mahatma by knowledge; a master knows as the result of thinking, and knowledge follows thought. A mahatma knows before he thinks, and thought is used only as the working out and applying of knowledge. The faculties of the mind are used by mahatmas and masters in any of the worlds, but only a mahatma may have full and free use of the light faculty and the I-am faculty. A mahatma uses the light and I-am faculties singly or together, with or apart from the other five faculties.

Each faculty has a special function and power, and is represented in each other faculty. Each faculty has not only its own function and power, but may be empowered by the other faculties, though all the others are dominated by the faculty to whose power they contribute.

The light faculty is the giver of light through all the manifested worlds. But the light of one world is not the light of another world. In its own world, the spiritual world, the light faculty is pure and unmixed intelligence, or the faculty through which intelligence comes and through which intelligence is expressed. The light faculty of the mind is the faculty through which the universal mind is perceived, and the faculty by or through which the individual mind becomes united with the universal mind.

By the aid of the light faculty, the time faculty reports truly the nature of time. The light faculty enables the time faculty to conceive and report matter truly in its ultimate and atomic combinations. By the light faculty acting with the time faculty all manner of calculations may be made. In the absence of the light faculty, the time faculty cannot truly conceive nor report the changes of matter, the mind is inaccurate and cannot make any calculations nor have any true notion of time.

The light faculty acting with the image faculty enables the mind to give shape to unformed matter, to picture mentally an image or combination of images and forms in harmonious relationships, according to the power of the light which is perceived and by which light the forms are harmoniously shaped.

By the light faculty acting with the focus faculty, the mind is able to direct its attention to any subject or thing, to bring into range of consideration any mental problem, and by the light faculty the focus faculty is enabled to hold steadily and estimate truly all forms, subjects or things. By the light faculty, the focus faculty is enabled to show the way to any attainment. In proportion to the absence of the light faculty the focus faculty cannot truly show to the mind the subject or thing to which it is directed.

The light faculty of the mind acting on the dark faculty, causes the mind to become conscious of its own ignorance. When the dark faculty is used under the light faculty, falsehoods and all untruthfulness are brought to light and the mind may find all imperfections, absurdities and disproportion, concerning whatever subject or thing it is directed to. But if the dark faculty is used without the light faculty, it produces confusion, ignorance and mental blindness.

By the light faculty acting with the motive faculty, the mind can know the causes of all events, actions or thoughts, and may decide or predict truly what will result from any thought or action. By the light and the motive faculties, the guiding principle of one's life and action, the causes of anyone's actions and the results which will accrue therefrom may be known. By the light and the motive faculties acting harmoniously together, one is able to find his own motives and is able to decide and choose which motive shall be the guide of his future thoughts and actions. Without the light faculty, the motive faculty will not truly show the motives in one's self which prompt thought and action.

By the light faculty acting with the I-am faculty, the I-am-I becomes conscious of and may be known to itself. By the light acting with the I-am faculty man impresses his identity on all surrounding things and charges his I-am faculty on and into the atmosphere and personalities with which he comes in contact. By the light and I-am faculties, the mind is able to see itself throughout nature and to see all things evolving toward self-conscious individuality. In the absence or in proportion to the absence of the light faculty, the

I-am faculty is unable to distinguish itself in matter, and man is undecided and in doubt as to whether man has any future existence apart from his body.

The light faculty should act and be always present in the action of the other faculties. When the light faculty is absent or has ceased to function, man is spiritually blind.

The time faculty is the recorder of changes of matter in manifestation. By the time faculty the differences and changes in matter and phenomena are known. Time or the change of matter is different in each of the worlds. By the time faculty, time in any of the manifested worlds is comprehended in the world in which it is acting.

By the time faculty acting on the light faculty, the mind is able to look into the world to which it is directed and to perceive the proportion in which particles or bodies are related to each other and what is the period of their action in combination. By the time faculty acting on the light faculty, the light faculty may make clear to the mind, according to its power and purity, the duration of a cell and the relation and changes of its indivisible particles, and the mind may comprehend the relation and changes of the worlds in the duration of eternity. Without the function of the time faculty, the light faculty can show to the mind no changes in anything.

By the acting of the time faculty on the image faculty, the image faculty shows rhythm and meter and proportion in form, whether the form be considered as an etheric wave or ideal image to be chiselled from a marble column. When under the influence of the time faculty, the image faculty will reveal the succession of forms, how one form follows that which preceded it and ends in the one which follows it, throughout involution and evolution. In the absence of the time faculty, the image faculty can show no relation between forms, and the mind will be unable through the image faculty to make or recall or follow melody, meter, and harmony, or to see color in or give it to any subject.

The time faculty directed on the focus faculty shows the difference and proportion and relation of subject and object. By the aid of the time faculty the focus faculty can group and show the relation between things and events of any particular period. If the time faculty does not lend aid, the focus faculty is unable to gather all the matter relating to the subject to which it is directed and the mind is unable to estimate the subject in its true light.

Acting with the time faculty, the dark faculty may declare the succession and nature of desire, the measure and intensity of desire, and the transformations of desire. Under the influence of the time faculty, the dark faculty may show the different states and changes of sleep, its depths and their periods. If the time faculty does not act with the dark faculty, the dark faculty can have no regular action and is unable to follow any order in action.

By the action of the time faculty with the motive faculty, the cycles and their changes may be known in any of the worlds, the causes of the groupings and actions of atoms, of international wars, or the peaceful combination and co-operation of nations. By use of the time faculty, the motive faculty will make known to the mind the effects which will follow the thinking of any thought and the action of that thought in the different worlds and the periods in which the events will occur. If the time faculty is inactive, the motive faculty cannot show the relation of cause to effect, and without the time faculty the mind will be confused and the motive faculty will be unable to distinguish cause from effect.

The I-am faculty acting under the influence of the time faculty spins and weaves out of matter webs and conditions and environments for the mind through the manifested worlds in, under and according to which it acts. By the use of the time faculty, the I-am faculty is able to trace the conditions and environments through which the mind has acted in any period of time. According to the inactivity of the time faculty, the I-am faculty is unable to recall its relation to any period or event and is unable to see itself as existing in the past or the future. The time faculty must be present in all mental activities and operations of men.

The image faculty is the matrix in which matter is held and given outline and form. Through the image faculty, forms last.

The image faculty acting with the light faculty causes the mind to picture forms in color and in the quality of the world in which it acts. Without the image faculty the light faculty can show no distinction in outline, nor difference in form.

By the image faculty acting on the time faculty, time, matter, is shaped and precipitated into form in the world in which it acts. With the image faculty the time faculty shows to the mind the forms which have been related or associated in the past. Without the image faculty the time faculty is unable to take and to come into form, in any of the three manifested worlds.

By the use of the image faculty the focus faculty can bring into view any of the forms of the past and show to the mind any form of the future which has already been outlined and determined. Without the image faculty, the focus faculty is unable to show forms to the mind.

By action of the image faculty on the dark faculty, the dark faculty causes to appear to the mind and take form, its fears, doubts, appetites and passions. By use of the image faculty the dark faculty causes the mind to see forms in the dream state. Without the image faculty, the dark faculty is unable to give shape to any fear or to see any forms in dreams.

By the image faculty the motive faculty makes the mind aware of the types and species of forms which result and how they result from different thoughts. Without the image faculty the motive faculty is unable to make known to the mind the forms which thoughts take, or to give form to ideals.

By the use of the image faculty, and through the I-am faculty, the mind may know the forms of its past incarnations, see the forms through which it had passed, or the form in which it now is in the psychic world, and its form in the mental world, and may comprehend what it as form is at the time in the spiritual world. By aid of the image faculty and through the I-am faculty, the mind is able to conceive its form in its own state as distinct from the form of the physical body.

In proportion to the absence of the image faculty, the I-am faculty is unable to picture to the mind any forms or designs relating to any of the worlds, or to have any form or style of expression. Without the image faculty acting with the other faculties the mind is unable to describe or picture to itself or other minds, other forms or its own in any of the worlds except that and at the time in which it is then acting, and it will be unable to see the beauty of form in figure or speech or grace in movement.

The focus faculty balances and relates the other faculties to each other. It gives a mental grasp of any subject and is that faculty by which the mind rises and descends from world to world. By the focus faculty the other faculties are drawn together and blended from world to world until they enter into the spiritual world where they all become one. When all the faculties are blended into one, the mind is knowledge and power, radiant and immortal.

When the light faculty is directed or induced by the focus faculty the mind is illuminated on any subject in the world to which it is directed. As the light faculty is aided by the focus faculty, the mind is able to surround itself with a body of light other than that of the world in which it is acting. By aid of the focus faculty the light faculty brings light to a center and makes a body of light. In the absence of the focus faculty, the light faculty diffuses light without relation to subjects or objects.

The time faculty acted on by the focus faculty enables the mind to find any event in the world of its action and to trace the consecutive periods of time, matter, in its revolutions, and to calculate the succession of changes from world to world. With the aid of the focus faculty the time faculty may be made to increase or decrease the flow of time and to show how time passes from one world into the other and becomes the time of that other. Without the focus faculty the time faculty is unable to report to the mind any occurrence of the past, and the mind is not able to see any change that may come about in the future, and the mind is unable to calculate concerning the past or future.

Acted on by the focus faculty the image faculty may reproduce any form that has existed anywhere. By the focus faculty acting on the image faculty the mind is able to magnify infinitely the minutest forms, and reduce those of greatest magnitude to the infinitely small. In the absence of the focus faculty, the image faculty cannot show to the mind any distinct objects or forms, nor can it give mental perspective to figures.

Under the influence of the focus faculty, the dark faculty may suspend the activities of the mind on the physical plane of action, and produce sleep, or it may produce a hypnotic sleep of other minds, or it may keep one's self awake and awaken others from a hypnotic sleep. Under the influence of the focus faculty the dark faculty can make known to the mind, darkness and the nature of sleep, what death is, and the processes of death. Under the direction of the focus faculty, the dark faculty can be made to report each of one's desires and what one's ruling desire is, what the appetites are, what passions, anger and the vices are, and how they affect the other faculties of the mind, and it can show the manner of the action between the faculties and the senses. In the absence of the focus faculty the dark faculty suspends the action of the other faculties of the mind, and produces sleep. When the focus faculty ceases to act with the dark faculty, the dark faculty produces death.

By directing the focus faculty on the motive faculty, one is able to know the governing principle of his own life or in the lives of others. With the focus faculty the motive faculty will make known the motive which caused any thought, action or result and judge the consequences resulting therefrom. By aid of the focus faculty, the motive faculty will show what thought is, what prompts it, and where it dwells. Without the focus faculty motives cannot be known, thought cannot be discovered and the mind cannot know the causes of its action.

The I-am faculty by the correct use of the focus faculty makes known to the mind who and what it is. It is able to know and preserve its identity in any of the worlds, irrespective of the conditions under which it might act. But according to the inability of the I-am to use the focus faculty the mind will not know itself in any of the worlds. In the absence of the focus faculty, the faculties cannot act in combination, and insanity follows. The focus faculty preserves a unity in the action of the faculties. If the focus faculty is not used in connection with each and all of the faculties no one singly or in combination can give true reports concerning any subject or thing.

The influence of the dark faculty extends through all the worlds and affects all other faculties of the mind. The dark faculty is the cause of all doubt and fear in the mind. If not dominated, checked or controlled by one or all of the other faculties, the dark faculty will produce riot and confusion in the mind. The dark faculty is negatively strong and resists control or domination. It is under control only in so far as it is made to perform its functions in the service of the other faculties. The dark faculty is a necessary and valuable servant when mastered, but a strong, ignorant and unreasoning tyrant when it is not controlled.

When acted on by the dark faculty, the light faculty is unable to make known to the mind any subject or thing in proportion to the strength of its action or resistance, and in proportion to its dominance the mind is blinded. In the absence of the dark faculty, all things could be seen by the mind, but there would be no periods of rest and activity, or day and night.

Under the action of the dark faculty, the time faculty can not report orderly changes and is unable to make calculations concerning periods or events. In proportion as the dark faculty ceases to control or influence the time faculty, the time periods are lengthened and when the dark faculty does not act at all, time disappears into eternity and all is a day of negative bliss, because there would be no shade or contrast to the light which would then prevail and the mind would make no calculations.

The image faculty acted on by the dark faculty is unable to give form to anything or it will reproduce all the forms of darkness of which the mind had ever been aware, and the dark faculty will cause the image faculty to produce new images, new forms of ungainly or hideous and malignant aspects, representing the phases of desires and passions and sensuous vices. In the absence of the dark faculty, the image faculty would show forms of beauty, and picture to the mind those things which are pleasing to the mind.

In proportion to the influence of the dark faculty, the focus faculty is unable to present to the mind any subject or thing, cannot draw into view or relate to each other thoughts and the subjects of thought, nor co-ordinate or relate the action of the faculties to each other. In the absence and quiescence of and control over the dark faculty, the focus faculty can group and co-ordinate objects, thoughts and the subjects of thought, and present them clearly and concisely to the mind. In the absence of the dark faculty the focus faculty is unable to temper and strengthen the mind. But while quiescent and controlled, the focus faculty enables the mind to be continuously conscious.

When dominated by the dark faculty, the motive faculty is unable to acquaint the mind with its motives or the causes of its action, and in proportion as the influence of the dark faculty prevails, the motive faculty is prevented from enabling the mind to understand the relation between cause and effect, the manner and method of thought and the mind is unable to distinguish between its faculties and the senses, and the causes of the actions of either. In the absence of or its control over the dark faculty, the motive faculty can make known to the mind its own nature and enables the mind to choose and decide without doubt the best course of action.

In proportion to the influence and prevalence of the dark faculty, the I-am faculty is unable to give the mind identity, and the mind ceases to be conscious in any or all of the worlds of its action. When the dark faculty prevails against the I-am faculty it causes the mind to become unconscious of and produces death in that world; in the absence of the dark faculty the I-am faculty becomes all-conscious in the world of its action; light prevails, but the mind has nothing to overcome, and having no resistance, by the overcoming of which it could gain strength, it can not become fully self-conscious and immortal. By the mastery of the dark faculty, the I-am faculty gains immortality and learns to know itself. In the absence of the dark faculty the faculties do not learn perfection in function, and their operations would become slower and finally cease; the mind would be simply conscious without individuality and without being conscious of consciousness.

By means of the motive faculty, the mind causes all action and the results of action; and starts action of the other faculties. The motive faculty is the cause of their acting and determines their power. By the motive faculty, the mind decides upon its ideals and what its attainment shall be.

By the motive faculty the mind decides on what subject or object the light faculty will illuminate it. In proportion to the absence of the motive faculty the light faculty cannot inform and the mind cannot understand the spiritual world, the nature of light.

By the motive faculty, the time faculty makes known to the mind the nature and action of time, or matter, in any of the manifested worlds; it shows the causes of its circulations, determines the periods of its action and decides the quantity and quality and proportion of its action. With the aid and according to the development of the motive faculty, the time faculty can report to the mind any occurrence or event of the past, however distant, understand the present and predict the events of the future, in so far as they have been determined by a motive. By the motive faculty the time faculty can show to the mind the nature of thought, the method and manner of its action on other matter, and how and why it guides or directs matter into form. When the motive faculty is inactive, the time faculty is unable to report or make known to the mind the nature of matter, the cause of its changes and how and why it comes and goes and changes in regular periods.

By the motive faculty through the image faculty are decided the various kinds of figures, forms, features, colors and appearance in any of the manifested worlds, or what these will be in the spiritual world, and whether they will or will not be according to proportion of the ideal. By the motive faculty acting through the image faculty, figure and color and form is given to thought, and thought takes form. Without the aid of the motive faculty the image faculty of the mind cannot give form to matter.

When the motive faculty acts on the focus faculty there is determined when, where and under what conditions the mind will incarnate, and it is decided and regulated what one's karma will be. By the motive faculty is determined birth in the physical world and how and under what conditions the mind will be born into any of the other worlds. By aid of the motive faculty, the mind is able to find through the focus faculty its motives and to know causes. In the absence of the motive faculty, the worlds cannot start into operation, matter has no impetus to action, the mind has no purpose in effort, its faculties remain inert and the machinery of karma cannot be set in action.

According to the action of the motive on the dark faculty, the dark faculty is aroused into action; it resists, beclouds and confuses the mind; it is the cause of inordinate appetites, and produces passion and all phases of desire; it suggests and stimulates all longings, wishes and ambitions. On the other hand, it is the means of controlling the appetites and passions, and is the cause of noble aspirations, according to the motive which governs the dark faculty. With the motive faculty acting through the dark faculty, the mind is cut off from the physical world and death is produced; and, according to the motive, the mind is detained by the dark faculty of desire, after death. According to the motive, the mind is born from its physical body through the dark faculty into the mental world. In the absence of the dark faculty the mind would have no means of overcoming resistance and it could not achieve any attainments nor self-conscious immortality.

By the motive faculty acting on the I-am faculty, the mind decides of what it will become conscious, and by being conscious what it will become, determines what the quality of its reflective powers will be and what it will reflect.

The motive faculty acting on the I-am faculty decides what the mind will do and sense and think and know when acting in the physical and the other worlds. The motive faculty determines why and for what purpose the mind seeks immortality, the method by which immortality will be attained, and what the mind will be and do after immortality. According as the motive faculty guides the

I-am faculty, the mind will or will not misunderstand or mistake itself for its bodies, will or will not know right from wrong action, will or will not be able to judge circumstances and conditions at their true value, and to know itself as it is at any time in any of the worlds, and also what it may become in this and in future periods of manifestation. If the motive faculty is absent, there is no self action of the mind. The motive faculty must be present in all mental functions and action. Only by learning its motives can the mind know its true self.

The I-am is the self-conscious, self-identifying and individualizing faculty of the mind.

The I-am faculty gives individuality to and individualizes light. By the I-am faculty acting with the light faculty, the mind becomes a sphere of splendor and power and glory. By the I-am acting with the light faculty, the mind may remain in the spiritual world, or may appear as a superior being to any of the beings of the worlds in which it may enter. In the absence of the I-am faculty, light remains universal and not individualized, self knowledge is impossible and mind can have not identity.

The I-am faculty of the mind acting through the time faculty impresses matter with identity, gives to the mind continuity and preserves identity of self through change. In the absence of the I-am faculty, mind cannot assimilate simple matter, and matter can not become self-conscious.

By the action of the I-am faculty through the image faculty the mind dominates, holds and gives distinctness to form. It impresses the idea of I-am-ness on forms and shows the way by which forms evolve and by which progress toward individuality can be made; it determines species and type; it numbers, names and preserves order and species of and in form. Through the image faculty, the I-am faculty determines in one physical life what the form of its next physical body shall be. In the absence of the I-am faculty, the image faculty can give no distinctness nor individuality to form; matter would remain simple and uniformed and there would be no forms.

Through the focus faculty the I-am faculty gives power. The I-am faculty acting through the focus faculty speaks itself out of, through and into each of the worlds. By the I-am acting through the focus faculty, the mind is equilibrated, balanced, adjusted and related to its bodies and can be in and act and know itself through all the worlds and as distinct from its body of each of the worlds. By the I-am acting with the focus faculty, the mind may locate and find itself in any of the worlds. By the action of the I-am with the focus faculty, the mind has memory. In the absence of the I-am faculty the human form would be an idiot. Without the I-am faculty the focus faculty would become inactive and the mind would be unable to leave the world in which it is.

By the I-am faculty acting on the dark faculty, the mind resists, exercises, trains and educates desire and overcomes ignorance, regulates its appetites, silences and transmutes its vices into virtues, dominates darkness, conquers and overcomes death, perfects its individuality and becomes immortal. In the absence of or without control by the I-am faculty, the dark faculty would control or suppress and crush out or cause to become inactive the other faculties of the mind, and the mind would suffer mental and spiritual death.

By the action of the I-am on the motive faculty, the mind becomes impressed with the idea of egotism, which is the dominant motive of its action. As I-am dominates the motives, the mind will have an uneven development and imperfect and inharmonious attainment. As motive decides the action of the I-am faculty, the mind will become evenly developed, harmonious in its action and have perfect attainment. Without the I-am faculty acting with the motive faculty, the mind would have no comparison for action and no idea of attainment.

The I-am faculty should act with all other faculties of the mind. It conveys the idea of permanence to the other faculties and is the end of attainment as mind. Without the I-am faculty, there would be no continuity, permanence nor individuality of the mind.

(To be continued)

ADEPTS, MASTERS AND MAHATMAS

(Continued)

[From *The Word,* Vol. 11 No. 5, August 1910]

THE faculties do not act singly and independently of each other, but in combination. When one attempts to use one of the faculties exclusively, the mind is inharmonious in its action and will not be even in its development. Only when all act together and in their proper functions and capacities, will the mind have the best and fullest development. The faculties are as organs to the mind. By them, it comes in contact with the worlds, takes in, changes, assimilates, transforms matter into itself and acts on and changes the matter of the worlds. As the senses serve the body, so the faculties serve the mind. As sight, hearing, and the other senses aid each other, and contribute to each other's action for the general welfare, economy and preservation of the body, so the faculties should act with and contribute to each other's action in the exercise, training and development of the mind as a whole; and as the well preserved and well ordered body is an important and valuable servant to the mind, so is the mind, with well trained, developed and articulated faculties, a valuable and important servant to humanity and the worlds. As great care through long years of effort must be exercised in training and perfecting the senses of the body, so also should great care be exercised in the use and development of the faculties of the mind. As loss or impairment of any of the senses affect the value and power of the body, so will impairment of the action of the faculties limit the action of the mind.

All men use their senses, but only by training and development can the greatest or best use be made of them. All men use their faculties, but few consider differences and distinctions between the faculties themselves, and between the faculties of the mind and the senses of the body. An artist becomes great in proportion to the ability to use his senses. A mind becomes great and useful to the degree that it develops, and co-ordinates its faculties.

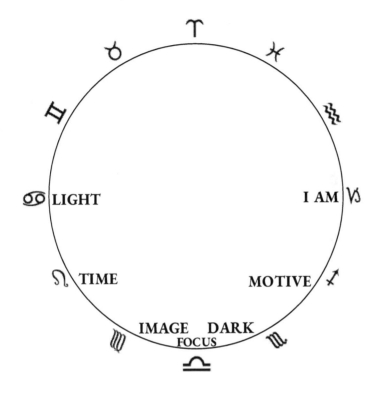

FIGURE 35
*The Faculties of the Mind and the Signs of
the Zodiac to Which They Correspond*

A man becomes a master when he has learned how to use his faculties. A master alone is able to use his faculties at all times intelligently and to know them as distinct from his senses, but every man uses the faculties of his mind in some degree. From the time one begins to exercise and develop his faculties and to control by them his senses, from that time, consciously or unconsciously to himself, does he begin to become a master. A man's body has special organs through which the senses act, so also are there centers and parts of the human body through which and from which the faculties of the mind act and are operated while the mind is in the body.

One who would become an artist knows that he needs and must use the organs of the senses, upon which his art rests. He knows that he must care for that part of his body through which he develops his sense; yet he does not give his eye or ear special treatment; he trains it by exercise. As he measures tones and distances and compares colors and forms and estimates proportions and harmonies, his senses become keener and answer more readily to his call, until he excels in his particular art. Though it may not be known to him, he must, to be proficient in his art, exercise his faculties. He is using his faculties, but in the service of the senses, which is what those do who are in the school of the senses. Rather should he use his senses in the service of his mind and its ministers, the faculties.

The eye does not see, nor the ear hear shades of color and tone, form and rhythm. The senses, through the eye or ear, sense the color or form or sound, but they cannot analyze, compare nor reason about them. The light and time faculties do this and they do it under the name of the senses of sight or sound, and not under the name of the faculties of light and time. So that the senses gain honor not due to them and they masquerade as the faculties, but these serve the senses. By training the faculties to serve the senses and by recognizing the senses as the things to be honored, the way is found which leads to the school of the senses, that of the adepts.

Considering the faculties as distinct from and superior to the senses, and training one's self to know the faculties and their working as distinct from the senses, and letting the faculties control the senses, is the way leading to the school of the mind, which is the school of the masters.

The faculties of the mind can be trained in a way similar to the way in which the senses are trained. As with the senses, the way to train the faculties is by exercising them. They must be exercised independently of the senses. While the faculty is developed which corresponds to the sense of sight, the eye and the sense of sight should not be used. Only after the practice in the training of the light faculty has met with enough success to warrant assurance in its independent use, only then may the eye be used in connection with it. But even then the organ of sight as well as the sense of sight must be considered and understood as subordinate to the light faculty. One does not exercise nor develop the light faculty by sitting with his eyes closed and trying to see things. If one sees things with his eyes closed, he is developing his inner, clairvoyant or astral sense of sight, and not the light faculty. The faculties are trained by mental processes and not by the senses or their organs. The senses should not be keyed up as by gazing fixedly with the eyes closed, or by straining the ear to hear. The senses should be relaxed, not keyed up.

One should begin to train the faculties by a certain attitude of mind. To train the light faculty, the attitude should be of attention, confidence, sincerity and good will.

The light of the light faculty is intelligence, which comes and illuminates the mind according to one's progress. To develop this faculty of the mind, one may direct his mind to the subject of light and try to perceive and understand what is light in each of the worlds, spiritual, mental, psychic and physical. As one becomes proficient in the exercise, he will find that intelligence is a light and will illuminate the mind when the light faculty is able to perceive it.

The attitude of mind to exercise the time faculty is of patience, endurance, exactitude and harmony. All the faculties should be directed in thought to the subject of time and the time faculty. As one develops in the practice of these four virtues, the mind will become enlivened, stimulated, and a change will come in the understanding of things, and change itself will have new meanings.

To seek co-ordination, proportion, dimension and beauty, should be the attitude of mind when one wants to exercise the image faculty. The energies of the mind should be directed to the idea of the image faculty, but no pictures or forms should be created by the mind while the image faculty is being called mentally into operation. If pictures or colors or figures are outlined and seen, the clairvoyant sense of sight is being developed and not the image faculty. To assist in the calling of the image faculty into independent use, words, names and numbers should be conceived and their beauty and proportion, dimension and co-ordination should be seen, as the names, numbers and words are formed or imaged.

Seeking balance, justice, duality and unity is the mental attitude or condition in which one should be for the exercise of the focus faculty, and with this attitude he should bend all his faculties to know that which he values above all things. The subject which is taken must, however, not be anything connected with the senses or possible to be reached by sensuous perception. As he advances in his practice his mind will become clearer, the mental fog will be removed and he will be illuminated on the subject of his search.

Strength, service, love and sacrifice should constitute the attitude in which one should attempt the exercise and training of the dark faculty. He should try to be informed concerning the secret of death. As he preserves the right attitude of mind and continues the exercise, he will understand it.

Freedom, action, honesty and fearlessness, should be the qualities making up the mental attitude necessary for the exercise and training of the motive faculty. All of the energies of the mind should be centered on knowing the action of right thought. With this purpose in mind the exercise should be continued and the success will be announced when one's true nature is revealed to him. All of these qualities are necessary to face one's true nature. But the man exercising this faculty should determine and have the earnest desire and firm resolve to right wrongs at any cost. If this intention is certain and persistent in his mind, he will not fear.

Permanence, knowledge, self and power, form the attitude in which the mind can, with all faculties bent on the subject of self, try to call into independent, conscious being, the I-am faculty. In proportion to the success achieved, the mind will receive an accession of power, and man a confidence in his persistence through death, and he may at his will stand forth as a column of light.

The parts of the body through which the focus faculty operates during normal activities have been given. In order to exercise and discipline the faculties, it is not actually necessary to know all correspondences of the parts of the body with which they are connected, nor the centers from which they are operated. The parts and centers will become apparent to those who are able to use them. As the faculties are understood and their action becomes clear to one's thought, he will of himself find the way to exercise, discipline and use them as naturally as he learns to speak and think and give expression to his thought. It is not necessary to have a teacher or a master. One learns by aiding himself and he is assisted in his efforts to the degree that he finds the means to aid himself.

Outside his own heart, there is no place at which an aspirant to discipleship in the school of the masters may apply for admission, and no person is able to receive or accept such aspirant, nor is anyone able to introduce him to a master. The school of the masters is the school of the world. There are no favorites. Each disciple must depend on his merits and is accepted by no preference nor because of credentials. The only speech which the masters can hear and respond to are the thoughts and aspirations of the heart. One's thoughts may be hidden to one's own view, but they speak their true nature in no uncertain notes, where thoughts are words.

The age is ripe for those who will to appoint themselves disciples in the school of the masters. The appointment can be made in no other way than by one's resolution. Most people are willing to be masters, as they are willing to be great men and leaders of civilization, but few are willing to fit themselves and comply with the requirements. Those who make rash promises, who expect much in a short time, who look for results and advantages within some fixed time, who think that they may practice on other people and who promise the world to give it an uplift, will do others little good and be themselves the least benefited. One cannot appoint himself as disciple to another whom he opines to be a master, nor to a society or group of people, and have the appointment result in permanent good to any concerned. Masters do not hold their lodges with men. There are lodges, societies and groups of people who do accept pupils and do give secret instructions and who do have occult practices, but these are not the masters spoken of in the preceding pages.

When one appoints himself a disciple in the school of the masters, he shows that he does not understand what this means if he sets a time for his acceptance. His self appointment should be made only after due consideration and in a calm moment, and when he has an understanding that he is in eternity and that he makes the appointment for eternity, and not subject to time. When one so appoints himself, he will live on confidently, and although the years may roll by without his seeing any other evidence than his moral improvement and increase of mental strength, still he knows he is on the way. If he does not, he is not made of the right stuff. One who is of the right stuff cannot fail. Nothing will daunt him. He knows; and what he knows no one can take away.

There are no great things for one to do who would be a disciple, but there are many little things to do which are of the greatest importance. The little things are so simple that they are not seen by those who look about to do great things. But no great thing can be done by the disciple except by nurture of the small.

Cleanliness and food are simple subjects and these he must understand. Of course he will keep his body clean and wear clean garments, but it is more important that his heart be clean. Cleanliness of heart is the cleanliness here meant. Cleanliness of heart has been advised for ages. In every sphere of life it has been advised. If a student of occult lore makes light of it, let him know that a clean heart is not a metaphor; it is a physical possibility and may be made a physical fact. A self appointed disciple becomes an accepted disciple in the school of the masters, when he learns how and begins to cleanse his heart. Many lives may be needed to learn how to begin to clean the heart. But when one knows how and begins to clean his heart, he is no longer uncertain about it. Once he has learned the work as an accepted disciple, he knows the way and he proceeds with the cleansing. The cleansing process covers the entire period of discipleship.

When the disciple has his heart clean, his work as disciple is done. He passes through death while living and is born a master. His heart is needed for his birth. He is born out of his heart. After he is born out of it, he still lives in it, but is master of it. While he lives in his heart he lives with the laws of time, though he has overcome time. A strong heart is needed. Only a clean heart is strong. No drugs, sedatives, or tonics will avail. Only one specific, one simple, is needed. No apothecary, nor any cult or organization, with or without quick cures or sure ones, can supply it. This simple is: Simple Honesty. One must be his own physician and he must find it. It may have been long unnoticed, but it can be found in the heart. It may take a long search to find it, but when it is found and used, the results will repay the effort.

But honesty in the gross, the kind which the legal and even moral codes of the world demand, is not the simple which the disciple needs. Much of the gross is needed to get a little of the essence, in the simple. When honesty is applied to the heart, it changes the heart. The treatment will be sure to hurt, but will do it good. Only one who tries, knows the difficulties and obstacles encountered and the strength needed to find and use honesty. Those who are already honest, and are always offended at having their honesty questioned, need not try.

When a little of the specific of honesty is by an aspirant applied to his heart, he begins to stop lying. When he begins to stop lying, he begins to speak truly. When he begins to speak truly he begins to see things as they are. When he begins to see things as they are, he begins to see how things should be. When he begins to see how things should be, he tries to make them so. This he does with himself.

(To be concluded)

ADEPTS, MASTERS AND MAHATMAS

(Concluded)

[From *The Word,* Vol. 11 No. 6, September 1910]

WITH the subject of cleanliness, one learns about the subject of food. One who would enter the school of the masters must learn what are his needs of food, and what the kind and quantity which should be taken. The kind of food which he needs, to begin with, will depend upon his digestive and assimilative powers. Some get only a little nurture from much food. A few are able to get much nurture from little food. A man need not bother whether uncracked wheat, flaked rice, meat, fish or nuts, is the proper food for him. Honesty will tell him what he needs to eat. The kind of food needed for one self appointed in the school of the masters is of words and thoughts.

Words and thoughts are too simple for most people, but they will do for the disciple. They are what he needs. Words and thoughts are the food which one can make use of in the beginning and words and thoughts will be used ages hence, when he is more than human. At present, words are of little value and are only empty sounds, and thoughts can find no lodgment, and pass undigested through the mind. As one studies words and learns their meaning, they are to him as food. As he is able to see new things and old things in the words, he takes new mental life. He begins to think, and delights in thought as his food. He has new uses for his mental digestive tract.

At present, the minds of men are unable to digest words and assimilate thoughts. But to do this is incumbent on one who would be a disciple. Words and thoughts are his diet. If one cannot create them himself he must use such as he has. The mind takes, circulates, digests and assimilates its food by reading, listening, speaking, and thinking. Most people would object to take drugs and poisonous and indigestible stuff as food with their soups, salads and meats, lest that might cause injury and require the doctor; but they will read with avidity the latest yellow novel and family paper, with its rapes, murders, crookedness, corruption and abject worship of wealth and fashion's latest excrescence. They will listen to slander and slander others, enjoying gossip over the tea or card table, at the opera or after church, and they will spend odd moments in planning social conquests, or think out new business ventures just inside the limits of law; this through the greater portion of the day, and at night their dreams are of what they have heard and thought and done. Many good things are done and there have been many kind thoughts and pleasant words. But the mind does not thrive on too mixed a diet. As a man's body is made up of the food he eats, so a man's mind is made up of the words and the thoughts which he thinks. One who would be a disciple of the masters needs simple food of plain words and wholesome thoughts.

Words are the creators of the world, and thoughts are the moving spirits in them. All physical things are seen to be words, and thoughts are alive in them. When one has learned somewhat of the subjects of cleanliness and food, when he is able to distinguish somewhat of the difference between his personality and the being who inhabits it, his body will have a new meaning for him.

Men are already in a measure conscious of the power of thought and they are using it, though rashly. Having found the giant power, they delight in seeing it do things, not questioning the right. It may cost much pain and sorrow before it is realized that thought can work harm as well as good, and more harm than good will be done by using thought as a moving power unless the processes of thought are known, the laws governing them obeyed, and those using that power are willing to keep a clean heart and tell no lie.

Thought is the power which causes man to live from life to life. Thought is the cause of what man is now. Thought is the power which creates his conditions and environment. Thought provides him with work and money and food. Thought is the real builder of houses, ships, governments, civilizations, and the world itself, and thought lives in all these. Thought is not seen by the eyes of man. Man looks through his eyes at the things which thought has built; he may see thought living in the things which it has built. Thought is a constant worker. Thought is working even through the mind that cannot see the thought in the things which it has built. As man sees thought in things, thought becomes ever more present and real. Those who cannot see the thought in things must serve their apprenticeship until they can, then they will become workers and later masters of thought instead of being driven blindly by it. Man is the slave of thought, even while he thinks himself its master. Huge structures appear at the command of his thought, rivers are changed and hills removed at his thought, governments are created and destroyed by his thought, and he thinks he is the master of thought. He disappears; and he comes again. Again he creates, and again disappears; and as often as he comes he will be crushed, until he learns to know thought and to live in the thought instead of its expression.

The brain of man is the womb in which he conceives and bears his thoughts. To know thought and the nature of thought, one must take a subject of thought and think about it and love it and be true to it, and work for it in the legitimate way which the subject itself will make known to him. But he must be true. If he allows his brain to entertain subjects of thought unfavorable to the one of his choice, he will be the lover of many and will cease to be the real lover of the one. His progeny will be his ruin. He will die, for thought will not have admitted him into its secret. He will not have learned the true power and purpose of thought.

One who will think only when and as long as he pleases to think, or one who thinks because it is his business to think, does not in reality think, that is, he does not go through the process of forming a thought as it should be formed, and he will not learn.

A thought goes through the process of conception, gestation and birth. And when one conceives and carries a thought through gestation and brings it to birth, then he will know of the power of thought, and that a thought is a being. To give birth to a thought, one must take a subject of thought and must ponder over it and be true to it, until his heart and his brain give warmth to it and arouse it. This may take many days or many years. When his subject responds to his brooding mind, his brain is quickened and he conceives the subject. This conception is as illumination. The subject is known to him, so it seems. But he does not yet know. He has only a germ of knowledge, the quickened germ of a thought. If he does not nurture it the germ will die; and as he fails to nurture germ after germ he will at last be unable to conceive a thought; his brain will become barren, sterile. He must go through the period of gestation of the thought and bring it to the birth. Many men conceive and give birth to thoughts. But few men will bear them well and bring them well formed to the birth, and fewer still are able or will follow the process of the development of thought patiently, consciously and intelligently to its birth. When they are able to do so, they can sense their immortality.

Those who are unable to conceive a thought and follow it through all its changes and periods of development and watch its birth and growth and power, should not weaken their minds and keep them immature by useless regrets and idle wishes. There is a ready means by which they may become mature for thought.

The means by which one may make himself mature and fit for thought is, first, to procure and apply the cleansing simple to the heart, and at the same time to study words. Words mean little to ordinary man. They mean much to those who know the power of thought. A word is an embodied thought. It is a thought expressed. If one will take a word and fondle it and look into it, the word which he takes will speak to him. It will show him its form and how it was made, and that word which before was to him an empty sound will impart to him its meaning as his reward for calling it to life and giving it companionship. One word after the other he may learn. Lexicons will give him a passing acquaintance with words. Writers who can make them will put him on more familiar footing. But he himself must choose them as his guests and companions. They will become known to him as he finds delight in their company. By such means a man will become fit and ready to conceive and bear a thought.

There are many subjects of thought which should come into the world, but men are not yet able to give them birth. Many are conceived but few are properly born. Men's minds are unwilling fathers and their brains and hearts are untrue mothers. When one's brain conceives, he is elated and the gestation begins. But mostly the thought is still-born or abortive because the mind and the brain are untrue. The thought which was conceived and which was to have come into the world and been expressed in proper form, suffers death often because the one who was carrying it has turned it to his selfish ends. Feeling the power, he has prostituted it to his own designs and turned the power to work out his ends. So that those who might have brought into the world thoughts which would have been great and good, have refused them birth and brought forth monstrosities in their place which do not fail to overtake and crush them. These monstrous things find fruitful soil in other selfish minds and do great harm in the world.

Most people who think that they are thinking do not think at all. They cannot or do not give birth to thoughts. Their brains are only the fields where are prepared still-born thoughts and abortive thoughts or through which pass the thoughts of other men. Not many men in the world are really thinkers. The thinkers supply the thoughts which are worked over and built up in the fields of other minds. The things that men mistake and which they think they think, are not legitimate thoughts; that is, they are not conceived and given birth by them. Much of the confusion will cease as people think less about many things and try to think more about fewer things.

One's body should not be despised, nor should it be revered. It must be cared for, respected and valued. Man's body is to be the field of his battles and conquests, the hall of his initiatory preparations, the chamber of his death, and the womb of his birth into each of the worlds. The physical body is each and all of these.

The greatest and noblest, the most secret and sacred function which the human body can perform is to give birth. There are many kinds of birth which it is possible for the human body to give. In its present state it is able to give physical birth only, and is not always fit for that work. The physical body may also give birth to an adept body, and through the physical body may also be born the master body and the mahatma body.

The physical body is developed and elaborated in the pelvic region and born from the place of sex. An adept body is developed in the abdominal region and passes through the abdominal wall. A master body is carried in the heart and ascends through the breath. The mahatma body is carried in the head and is born through the roof of the skull. The physical body is born into the physical world. The adept body is born into the astral world. The master body is born into the mental world. The mahatma body is born into the spiritual world.

People of good sense who have seriously questioned the probability whether there are such beings as adepts, masters or mahatmas, but who now believe that necessity demands them and that they are probable, will indignantly object when being told that adepts are born through the abdominal wall, masters are born from the heart and that the mahatma is born through the skull. If there are adepts, masters and mahatmas they must get into existence in some way, but in a grand, glorious and superior way, and one becoming to beings of their power and splendor. But to think of their being born through the body of a friend or one's own body, the thought is shocking to one's intelligence and the statement seems unbelievable.

Those to whom this seems shocking cannot be blamed. It is strange. Yet physical birth is as strange as other births. But if they will go back in memory to the years of early childhood, perhaps they will recall that they then experienced a shock quite as severe. Their minds were little concerned with views of themselves and of the world around them. They knew that they were living and that they came from somewhere and were content in the thought until some other child explained, and then they were taunted or dared to ask mother. Those days have passed; we live in others now. Yet, though older, we are children still. We live; we expect death; we look forward to immortality. Like children, we suppose it will be in some miraculous way, but concern our minds little about it. People are willing to be immortal. The mind leaps at the thought. The churches of the world are monuments to the heart's desire for immortality. As when children, our modesty, good sense and learning feel shocked at hearing of births of immortal bodies. But the thought becomes easier as we grow older.

The disciple of the masters regards his body differently than when he was a child of the world. As he cleans his heart with honesty, and will not lie, his heart becomes a womb, and in purity of thought he conceives in his heart a thought; he conceives the master thought; that is the immaculate conception. At an immaculate conception the heart becomes a womb and has the functions of a womb. At such times the organs of the body bear a different relation to each other than at a physical conception. There is an analogous process in all manners of birth.

Physical bodies have seldom been conceived in purity. They have usually been—because conceived in unrighteousness—born in pain and fear, afflicted by disease and succumbed to death. Were physical bodies to be conceived in purity, carried through the period of gestation to birth in purity, and were then intelligently bred, there would live in them men of such physical might and power that death would find it hard to overtake them.

For physical bodies to be conceived in purity, both the man and woman must pass through a period of mental probation and bodily preparation before conception should be allowed. When the physical body is used for legitimatized or other prostitution, it is unfit to usher worthy human bodies into the world. For some time yet bodies will come into the world as they now do. Virtuous minds seek worthy bodies in which to incarnate. But all human bodies fashioned are for minds awaiting their readiness to enter. Different and worthy physical bodies must be ready and await the superior minds of the new race to come.

After physical conception and before the foetus has taken new life, it finds its nurture within its chorion. After it has found life and until birth, its food is supplied by the mother. Through her blood the foetus is fed from the heart of its mother.

At an immaculate conception there is a change in the relation of the organs. At the immaculate conception, when the heart has become the womb for the preparation of the master body, the head becomes the heart which feeds it. The master thought conceived in the heart is sufficient to itself until the growing body takes new life. Then the head, as the heart, must furnish the food which will bring the new body to birth. There is a circulation of thought between the heart and head as there is between the foetus and the heart of its mother. The foetus is a physical body and nourished by blood. The master body is a body of thought and must be nourished by thought. Thought is its food and the food by which the master body is fed must be pure.

When the heart is sufficiently cleansed it receives a germ fashioned of the quintessence of its life. Then there descends a ray through the breath which fecundates the germ in the heart. The breath which thus comes is the breath of the father, the master, one's own higher mind, not incarnate. It is a breath which is clothed in the breath of the lungs and comes into the heart and descends and quickens the germ. The master body ascends and is born through the breath.

The body of the mahatma is conceived in the head when the male and the female germs of the same body are there met by a ray from above. When this great conception takes place, the head becomes the womb where it is conceived. As in foetal development the womb becomes the most important organ in the body and the entire body contributes to its building up, so when the heart or head are acting as a womb the entire body is used primarily and principally to contribute to the support of the heart and head.

The heart and head of man are not yet ready to be the centers of operations for the body of a master or a mahatma. They are now centers from which are born words and thoughts. Man's heart or head are as wombs in which he conceives and gives birth to things of weakness, strength, beauty, power, love, crime, vice and all that is in the world.

The generative organs are the centers of procreation. The head is the creative center of the body. It can be used as such by man, but one who would make of it the womb of creation must respect and honor it as such. At present, men use their brains for purposes of fornication. When put to that use, the head is incapable of giving birth to great or good thoughts.

One who appoints himself as disciple in the school of the masters, and even to any noble purpose of life, may consider his heart or head as the fashioners and birthplaces of his thoughts. One who has pledged himself in thought to the immortal life, one who knows that his heart or head is the holy of holies, can no longer live the life of the sensuous world. If he tries to do both, his heart and head will be as places of fornication or adultery. The avenues leading to the brain are channels along which illicit thoughts enter for intercourse with the mind. These thoughts must be kept out. The way to prevent them is to clean the heart, choose worthy subjects of thought and to speak truthfully.

Adepts, masters and mahatmas may be taken as subjects of thought and they will be of benefit to the thinker and his race. But these subjects will be of benefit to those only who will use their reason and best judgment in the consideration. No statement made concerning this matter should be accepted unless it appeals to the mind and heart as true, or unless it is borne out and substantiated by one's experience and observation of life, and seems reasonable as in harmony with the future progress, evolution and development of man.

The preceding articles on adepts, masters and mahatmas may be of benefit to the man of good judgment, and they can do him no harm. They may also be of benefit to the rash man if he will heed the advice given and not attempt to do things which he infers from what he reads but which have not been written.

The world has been informed about adepts, masters and mahatmas. They will not press their presence upon men, but will wait until men can live and grow into it. And men will live and grow into it.

Two worlds seek entrance or recognition into the mind of man. Mankind is now deciding which of the worlds it will prefer: the astral world of the senses or the mental world of the mind. Man is unfit to enter either, but he will learn to enter one. He cannot enter both. If he decides for the astral world of the senses and works for that, he will come under the notice of the adepts, and in this life or those to come he will be their disciple. If he decides for the development of his mind he will as truly in time to come be recognized by the masters, and be a disciple in their school. Both must use their minds; but he of the senses will use his mind to get or produce the things of the senses and obtain entrance to the inner sense world, and as he tries to think of it and holds the thought in his mind and will work to gain entrance, the inner sense world, the astral world, will become more and more real to him. It will cease to be a speculation and may be known to him a reality.

He who would know the masters and enter the mental world must devote the power of his thought to the development of his mind, to calling into use the faculties of his mind independently of his senses. He should not ignore the inner sense world, the astral world, but if he senses it he should try to use his faculties until it disappears. In thinking and even by trying to think of the mental world, the mind becomes attuned to it.

Only a slight partition, a veil, divides man's thought from the mental world, and though it is ever present and his native realm, it seems strange, foreign, unknown, to the exile. Man will remain an exile until he has earned and has paid his ransom.

THE END

The following letter first appeared at the end of H. W. Percival's final editorial, "Ghosts." It is now included at the end of each book in a series of his editorials and "Moments With Friends" that was first published in 2022. The letter indicates that publication of The Word *would cease for the time being. The Word Foundation inaugurated a new series of* The Word *in 1986 for its members that continues to this day.*

To the Readers of *The Word*:

No further issues of *The Word* will be published for the present. But this number, which ends the Twenty-fifth Volume, is not expected to be the last. For the present, the publication of *The Word* will cease. The readers will be notified when *The Word* begins a new series.

Appreciation is due from all readers to the various contributors to *The Word.*

I have written an editorial for every published number of *The Word,* since my message was written in October, 1904 [*p. 1 in this book*], and have answered the questions in "Moments With Friends," which appeared from time to time. The editorials written by me were not signed with my name. Information not before given, so far as is known, will be found in these editorials and in some of the "Moments."

The main object of my writings was to bring the readers to an understanding and a valuation of the study of Consciousness, and to stimulate those who choose to become conscious of Consciousness. To that end a system has been made known by me. I have called it the Zodiac.

I would not state these facts, as to purpose and authorship, except that it is advisable, so as to guard against misrepresentation by some persons who have claimed and some who may claim to have found these teachings elsewhere than in *The Word,* and by some who attempt to change, distort or obscure what is stated in these Editorials. The information I have given in *The Word* is for those who will use it as a sacrifice to the plan of raising matter to Consciousness.

If *The Word* is taken up again it is my intention to write other articles. They will lead some of the Readers to know what it is to be Conscious of Consciousness.

HAROLD WALDWIN PERCIVAL

New York, April 15th, 1918

REPLICA OF "OUR MESSAGE"

The following is a photographic replica of Harold W. Percival's editorial "Our Message" from the first issue of his magazine *The Word*, published in October 1904.

" Unveil, O Thou : who giveth sustenance to the Universe; from whom all proceeds:
to whom all must return; that face of the true Sun, now hidden by a vase of golden light,
that we may see the TRUTH, and do our whole duty, on our journey to thy Sacred Seat."
THE GAIYATRI.

THE

WORD

VOL. 1   OCTOBER 21, 1904.   NO. 1.

OUR MESSAGE.

This magazine is designed to bring to all who may read
its pages, the message of the soul. The message is man is
more than an animal in drapings of cloth—he is divine, though
his divinity be masked by, and hidden in, the coils of flesh.
Man is no accident of birth nor plaything of fate. He is a
power, the creator and destroyer of fate. Through the power
within, he will overcome indolence, outgrow ignorance, and
enter the realm of wisdom. There he will feel a love for all
that lives. He will be an everlasting power for good.

A bold message this. To some it will seem out of place in
this busy world of change, confusion, vicissitudes, uncertainty.
Yet we believe it is true, and by the power of truth it will
live.

"It is nothing new," the modern philosopher may say,
"ancient philosophies have told of this." Whatever the philosophies of the past may have said, modern philosophy has
wearied the mind with learned speculations, which, continued
on the material line, will lead to a barren waste. "Idle imagination," says the scientist of our day of materialism, failing
to see the causes from which imagination springs. "Science

gives me facts with which I can do something for those living in this world." Materialistic science may make of deserts fertile pastures, level mountains, and build great cities in the place of jungles. But science cannot remove the cause of restlessness and sorrow, sickness and disease, nor satisfy the yearnings of the soul. On the contrary, materialistic science would annihilate the soul, and resolve the universe into a cosmic dust heap. "Religion," says the theologian, thinking of his particular belief, "brings to the soul a message of peace and joy." Religions, so far, have shackled the mind; set man against man in the battle of life; flooded the earth with blood shed in religious sacrifices and spilled in wars. Given its own way, theology would make of its followers, idol-worshippers, put the Infinite in a form and endow it with human weakness.

Still, philosophy, science, and religion are the nurses, the teachers, the liberators of the soul. Philosophy is inherent in every human being; it is the love and yearning of the mind to open and embrace wisdom. By science the mind learns to relate things to each other, and to give them their proper places in the universe. Through religion, the mind becomes free from its sensuous bonds and is united with Infinite Being.

In the future, philosophy will be more than mental gymnastics, science will outgrow materialism, and religion will become unsectarian. In the future, man will act justly and will love his brother as himself, not because he longs for reward, or fears hell fire, or the laws of man: but because he will know that he is a part of his fellow, that he and his fellow are parts of a whole, and that whole is the One: that he cannot hurt another without hurting himself.

In the struggle for worldly existence, men trample on each other in their efforts to attain success. Having reached it at the cost of suffering and misery, they remain unsatisfied. Seeking an ideal, they chase a shadowy form. In their grasp, it vanishes.

Selfishness and ignorance make of life a vivid nightmare and of earth a seething hell. The wail of pain mingles with the laughter of the gay. Fits of joy are followed by spasms of distress. Man embraces and clings closer to the cause of his sorrows, even while held down by them. Disease, the emissary of death, strikes at his vitals. Then is heard the message of the soul. This message is of strength, of love, of peace. This is the message we would bring: the strength to free the mind from ignorance, prejudice, and deceit; the courage to seek the truth in every form; the love to bear each other's burdens; the peace that comes to a freed mind, an opened heart, and the consciousness of an undying life.

Let all who receive "The Word" pass on this message. Each one who has something to give which will benefit others is invited to contribute to its pages.

INDEX

The Word Foundation

Declaration

The purpose of the Foundation is to make known the good news in the book *Thinking and Destiny* and other writings of the same author, that it is possible for the conscious self in the human body to nullify and abolish death by the regeneration and transformation of the structure of the human into a perfect and immortal physical body, in which the self will be consciously immortal.

The Human Being

The conscious self in the human body enters this world in a hypnotic dream, forgetful of its origin; it dreams through human life without knowing who and what it is, awake or asleep; the body dies, and the self passes out of this world without knowing how or why it came, or where it goes when it leaves the body.

Transformation

The good news is, to tell the conscious self in every human body what it is, how it hypnotized itself by thinking, and how, by thinking, it can dehypnotize and know itself as an immortal. In the doing of this it will change its mortal into a perfect physical body and, even while in this physical world, it will be consciously at one with its own Triune Self in the Realm of Permanence.

Concerning The Word Foundation

This is the time, when the newspapers and books show that crime is rampant; when there continue to be "wars and rumors of wars"; this is the time while the nations are distraught, and death is in the air; yes, this is the time for the establishment of The Word Foundation.

As declared, the purpose of The Word Foundation is for the vanquishing of death by the rebuilding and transformation of the human physical body into a body of immortal life, in which one's conscious self will find itself and return to The Realm of Permanence in The Eternal Order of Progression, which it left in the long, long ago, to enter this man and woman world of time and death.

Not everybody will believe it, not everybody will want it, but everybody should know about it.

This book and other like writings are especially for the few who do want the information and who are willing to pay the price which is in or by the regenerating and transforming of their bodies.

No human being can have conscious immortality after death. Each one must immortalize his or her own physical body to have immortal life; no other inducement is offered; there are no shortcuts or bargains. The only thing that one can do for another is to tell that other that there is the Great Way, as shown in this book. If it does not appeal to the reader he can dismiss the thought of eternal life, and continue to suffer death. But there are some people in this world who are determined to know the truth and to live the life by finding The Way in their own bodies.

Always in this world there have been individuals who disappeared unnoticed, who were determined to reconstruct their human bodies and to find their way to The Realm of Permanence, from which they departed, to come into this man and woman world. Each such one knew that the weight of the world's thought would hinder the work.

By the "world's thought" is meant the mass of people, who ridicule or distrust any innovation for improvement until the method advocated is proven to be true.

But now that it is shown that the great work can be done properly and reasonably, and that others have responded and are engaged in the "Great Work," the world's thought will cease to be a hindrance because The Great Way will be for the good of mankind.

The Word Foundation is for the proving of Conscious Immortality.

H. W. Percival

About the Author

As Harold W. Percival pointed out in the Author's Foreword of *Thinking and Destiny,* he preferred to keep his authorship in the background. His intention was that the validity of his statements not be influenced by his personality, but be tested according to the degree of self-knowledge within each reader. Nevertheless, people do want to know something about an author of note, especially if they are involved with his writings.

So, a few facts about Mr. Percival are mentioned here, and more details are available at thewordfoundation.org. The Author's Foreword of *Thinking and Destiny* also contains additional information, including an account of his experiences of being conscious of Consciousness. It was because of this noetic enlightenment that he was later able to know about any subject through a mental process he referred to as *real thinking*.

In 1912 Percival began to outline material for a book to contain his complete system of thinking. Because his body had to be still while he thought, he dictated whenever assistance was available. In 1932 the first draft was completed and was called *Thinking and The Law of Thought.* He did not give opinions or draw conclusions; rather, he reported that of which he was conscious through steady, focused thinking. The title was changed to *Thinking and Destiny,* and the book was finally printed in 1946. And so, the one-thousand-page masterpiece that provides crucial details on humankind and our relationship with the cosmos and beyond was produced over a period of thirty-four years. Subsequently, in 1951, he published *Man and Woman and Child* and, in 1952, *Masonry and Its Symbols: In the Light of* Thinking and Destiny, and *Democracy Is Self-*

Government. These three smaller books on selected subjects of importance reflect the principles and information contained in *Thinking and Destiny.*

Mr. Percival also published a monthly magazine, *The Word,* from 1904–1917. His inspired editorials were featured in each of 156 issues and earned him a place in *Who's Who in America.* The Word Foundation started a second series of *The Word* in 1986 as a quarterly magazine that is available to its members.

Harold Waldwin Percival was born on April 15, 1868 in Bridgetown, Barbados and passed away of natural causes on March 6, 1953 in New York City. His body was cremated according to his wishes. It has been stated that no one could meet Percival without feeling that he or she had met a truly remarkable human being, and his power and authority could be felt. For all his wisdom, he remained genteel and modest, a gentleman of incorruptible honesty, a warm and sympathetic friend. He was always ready to be helpful to any seeker, but never trying to impose his philosophy on anyone. He was an avid reader on diversified subjects and had many interests, including current events, politics, economics, history, photography, horticulture and geology. Besides his talent for writing, Percival had a propensity for mathematics and languages, especially classical Greek and Hebrew; but it was said that he was always prevented from doing anything but that which he was evidently here to do.

Other Books by Harold W. Percival

Thinking and Destiny

Many have found *Thinking and Destiny* to be unlike anything they have previously read. The author introduces us to the true meaning and purpose of Man, the Universe and Beyond. Provocative in its vast and detailed subject matter, the information may at first startle, or even elicit skepticism—until its contents have been absorbed. The statements made in this book are not based on speculation, dogma or religious authority. It was Percival's crucial experiences of the Presence of Consciousness as the Ultimate Reality that led to his ability to distill knowledge and truth from a process he called *real thinking*. Through this system of thinking he was able to provide sound answers to questions that heretofore have been considered by many to be unanswerable; such as, "Where did I come from?" and "Why am I here?" Mr. Percival stated that he was neither preacher nor teacher. He conveyed the information of which he was aware and left it to the individual to decide its veracity for him or herself. *Thinking and Destiny* is a guide for all humanity in a bewildering world. In print for over 75 years, this book is as relevant today as it will be for generations to come because the information is timeless and unaffected by prevalent thought. Reading this book may be one of your most profound and rewarding experiences.

Man and Woman and Child

This book, simply written, addresses humanity's descent into mortal bodies of birth and death. Here, you will learn the true identity of you—the conscious self in the body—and how you may break the hypnotic spell your senses and thinking have cast about you since childhood. Percival states: "These assertions are not based on fanciful hopes. They are substantiated by the anatomical, physiological, biological and psychological evidences given herein, which you can if you will, examine, consider and judge; and, then do what you think best."

Democracy Is Self-Government

Mr. Percival provides an original concept of "True" Democracy, where personal and national affairs are brought under the spotlight of eternal truths. This book sheds light on the direct connection between the conscious self in every human body and the affairs of the world in which we live. Percival tells us that we each have an opportunity, as well as a duty, to bring eternal Law, Justice, and Harmony to the world. This begins with learning to govern ourselves—our passions, vices, appetites, and behavior. "The purpose of this book is to point the way."—H. W. Percival

Masonry and Its Symbols: In the Light of Thinking and Destiny

Masonry and Its Symbols casts a new light on the age-old teachings and exalted purposes of Freemasonry. This ancient Order has existed under one name or another long before the building of the oldest pyramid. It is older than any religion known today! The author points out that Masonry is for humanity—for the conscious self in every human body. This book illuminates how any one of us can choose to prepare for the highest purposes of mankind—Self-knowledge, Regeneration and Conscious Immortality.

Monthly Editorials From THE WORD 1904–1917 Part I
Monthly Editorials From THE WORD 1904–1917 Part II

From 1904 to 1917, H. W. Percival published *The Word,* a monthly magazine of a philosophical nature that had a worldwide circulation. Over this thirteen-year period, each of the 156 issues contained one of his editorials. These two books contain the complete collection.

Moments With Friends From THE WORD 1906–1916

"Moments With Friends" is a question-and-answer feature of *The Word* magazine. Between 1906 and 1916, the questions listed in this book were posed by readers of *The Word* and answered by Mr. Percival under the appellation "A Friend."

Editorial Book Series by Topic from *The Word* 1904–1917

The following books present Percival's editorials by topic. Each of the books below is either on one topic, or on closely related topics. They are printed in a compact size of 5″ × 8″.

Brotherhood / Friendship
Christ / Christmas Light
Cycles / Birth-Death—Death-Birth
Glamour / Food / The Veil of Isis
Twelve Principles of the Zodiac
The Zodiac
I in the Senses / Personality / Sleep
Consciousness Through Knowledge
Psychic Tendencies and Development / Doubt
Karma
Mirrors / Shadows
Adepts, Masters and Mahatmas
Atmospheres / Flying
Hell / Heaven
Hope and Fear / Wishing / Imagination
Living / Living Forever
Intoxications
Ghosts

The following books are also available as
e-books from major booksellers:

Thinking and Destiny
Man and Woman and Child
Democracy Is Self-Government
Masonry and Its Symbols: In the Light of *Thinking and Destiny*
Monthly Editorials From THE WORD 1904–1917 Part I
Monthly Editorials From THE WORD 1904–1917 Part II
Moments With Friends From THE WORD 1906–1916

To learn more about Harold W. Percival's
books and other writings,
membership in The Word Foundation,
and our quarterly magazine, The Word, *please visit:*

thewordfoundation.org

Made in the USA
Columbia, SC
01 August 2024